W9-BEB-967

Storied City

A CHILDREN'S BOOK WALKING-TOUR GUIDE TO NEW YORK CITY

LEONARD S. MARCUS

Dutton Children's Books
NEW YORK

▪ *To George M. Nicholson* ▪

ACKNOWLEDGMENTS

A great many people helped in the making of *Storied City*. My thanks go to
the dedicated staffs of the New York Public Library, Brooklyn Public Library, and Queens Borough Public Library for responding to queries, verify-
ing facts, and offering useful suggestions along the way. Staff members at
numerous museums, historical societies, and other New York cultural and
civic institutions and city agencies also came to my aid, and I thank them
wholeheartedly as well. Most of all, I wish to express my deep appreciation
to my editor, Donna Brooks, and to everyone at Dutton Children's Books
who worked on *Storied City*. I thank them for understanding my idea from
the start, and for knowing how best to help me give that idea tangible form.

—L S M

Copyright © 2003 by Leonard S. Marcus
All rights reserved.

Library of Congress Cataloging-in-Publication Data
Marcus, Leonard S., date.
Storied city: a children's book walking-tour guide to New York City /
by Leonard S. Marcus.—1st ed.
p. cm.
ISBN 0-525-46924-9
1. New York (N.Y.)—Juvenile literature—Bibliography.   2. New York
(N.Y.)—In literature—Bibliography.   3. New York (N.Y.)—Guidebooks.
4. Children—Travel—New York (State)—New York—Guidebooks.
5. Literary landmarks—New York (State)—New York—Guidebooks.
I. Title.
Z1318.N5 M37 2003
[F128.33]
016.9747′1—dc21   2002069283

Published in the United States by Dutton Children's Books,
a division of Penguin Young Readers Group
345 Hudson Street, New York, New York 10014
www.penguinputnam.com

Designed by Sara Reynolds
Maps by Jason Henry and
Irene Vandervoort
Printed in USA
First Edition
1 3 5 7 9 10 8 6 4 2

CONTENTS

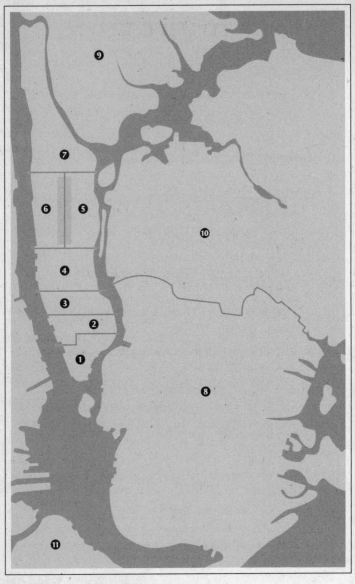

New York City Neighborhoods

1. Lower Manhattan
2. Greenwich Village / The East Village / SoHo
3. The Flatiron District / Gramercy Park / Chelsea
4. Midtown Manhattan
5. Central Park / Upper East Side
6. Central Park / Upper West Side
7. Harlem / Northern Manhattan
8. Brooklyn
9. The Bronx
10. Queens
11. Staten Island

INTRODUCTION

It'll be a great place if they ever finish it.
—O. HENRY, on the City of New York

*a*s a city of superlatives where people have long come
to follow their dreams, New York was bound to lodge itself in the world's imagination and to become a favorite
setting for literature. *Storied City* is a guide to more than
200 of the best books about New York written for young
people, from preschoolers to teens. It is also a walking-
tour guide to the city itself, pointing literary travelers—
those who live in New York as well as those who do
not—to dozens of specific sights that have lit the imagination of writers and artists as varied as E.B. White,
Maurice Sendak, Judy Blume, Faith Ringgold, Madeleine
L'Engle, Horatio Alger, and Kay Thompson.

The walking tours and excursions outlined in each
chapter can either be followed from start to finish or ab-
breviated to suit a reader's—or a family's—particular interests and circumstances. A stroll past the Greenwich
Village town house that Walter R. Brooks once called
home will have special appeal for Freddy the Pig fans. A
visit to Central Park's toy boat pond will beguile just
about anybody, whether or not they are old—or young—
enough to associate that magical place with *Stuart Little.*

Young readers of nonfiction will find titles that illumi-
nate a particular landmark's history or significance: both
a picture book and a young-adult biography of Mahatma
Gandhi, for instance, that tell the story of the Indian
leader whose poignant statue can be viewed in Union
Square; a photographic chronicle of immigrant life that
complements a visit to the Lower East Side.

Many destinations—the Manhattan Children's Museum and the Imagination Playground in Prospect Park
(Brooklyn), among others—maintain seasonal or year-
round schedules of children's book-related programs and
activities. Telephone numbers and web addresses have

been provided to help in planning a visit with these special events in mind. Suggestions offered throughout concerning public transportation options can be supplemented by visiting the Metropolitan Transportation Authority's excellent web site at: www.mta.nyc.ny.us or by phoning: 718-330-1234.

A bibliography of all recommended books, including their age categories, follows the main text. All but a few of the titles listed are in print as of this writing. Many featured authors and illustrators have created sequels and other New York–related books that, for reasons of space, could not be mentioned in these pages. New titles in the burgeoning mini-genre of books that involve New York City appear with each publishing season. Readers will want to continue their literary explorations on their own.

Storied City had its origins in an exhibition of New York–themed children's books that I co-curated, at the New York Public Library's Donnell Central Children's Room in the summer of 1995. While selecting the books for that exhibit, I was continually reminded of the power of words and images to encapsulate the essence of a place. Even more exciting was the discovery that each chosen book gained an added dimension simply by being seen in relation to the others. It was as though these varied volumes, each with its own story, had another, collective story to tell: they came together to form a virtual New York, both mirroring and taking off imaginatively from the real one.

It is with the greatest pleasure that I share both these New Yorks with you.

Stuart Little, *by E.B. White,*
illustrated by Garth Williams

Storied City

LOWER MANHATTAN

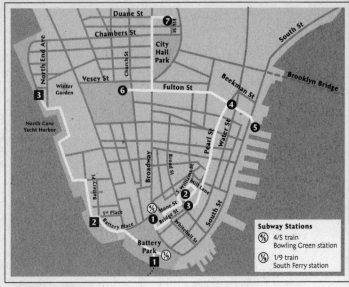

▲ **Walking Tour I**

❶ Bowling Green / National Museum of the American Indian

❷ Dutch Revival buildings (13-15 S. William St.)

❸ Fraunces Tavern Museum (54 Pearl St.)

❹ Bowne & Co. Stationers (211 Water St) / Beginning of South Street Seaport Museum area

❺ Piers 16 and 17

❻ World Trade Center Site

❼ African Burial Ground (corner of Duane and Elk St.)

▲ **Walking Tour II**

▪ Ellis Island National Monument and the Statue of Liberty National Monument (via ferry at Whitehall St. and Battery Park)

▪ Museum of Jewish Heritage (18 First Place, Battery Park City)

▪ Irish Hunger Memorial (corner of Vesey St. and North End Ave.)

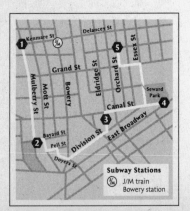

◀ **Walking Tour III**

❶ Corner of Kenmare and Mulberry St.

❷ Museum of Chinese in the Americas (70 Mulberry St. & Bayard)

❸ 17 Eldridge St. / K'Hal Adath Jeshurun (Eldridge St. Synagogue)

❹ Seward Park Library

❺ Lower East Side Tenement Museum (97 Orchard St.)

LOWER
MANHATTAN

The city of New York started out as a tiny trading post on the southern tip of Manhattan Island. In 1625, employees of the Dutch West India Company established the fortified post, called New Amsterdam, on land south of present-day Wall Street. Over the next decades, the ramshackle settlement grew to become a harbor town with Dutch-style stepped-gable brick facades, cobblestone streets, and even two canals. One of New Amsterdam's main thoroughfares—now lower Broadway—followed the path of an important Native American trading route.

As New Amsterdam expanded, relations with the region's Lenape people, who had first come to live in the region more than six thousand years earlier, turned from friendly to increasingly hostile and violent. Many Lenape died in armed skirmishes with the Dutch and of diseases unknown to them before the European settlers' arrival. The trickster-like tale of the Dutch purchase of Manhattan Island, in 1626, from the supposedly gullible Lenape for the equivalent of twenty-four dollars in trinkets and beads is, however, just folklore. No reliable record of the transaction has ever been discovered. The Lenape, in any case, had no concept of private property but believed the land was for all to share.

George Gustav Heye Center of the National Museum of the American Indian

WALKING TOUR I
Where New York City Began

We begin our tour at Bowling Green, an historic lower Manhattan crossroads, with a visit to the grand **George Gustav Heye Center of**

the National Museum of the American Indian (daily: 10 A.M.–5 P.M.; Thurs.: 10 A.M.–8 P.M.; 212-514-3700; www.americanindian.si.edu). The Heye Center is located directly across from the Bowling Green station of the Number 4 and 5 lines of the IRT subway. While this fascinating museum, a branch of the Smithsonian Institution, does not maintain a permanent exhibition devoted specifically to the original Native American peoples who lived in present-day New York, a visit here nonetheless serves as a fitting overture to an exploration of the city's beginnings.

The best introduction for readers aged 9 to 12 to the history and customs of the region's first inhabitants is JOSH WILKER's *The Lenape Indians* (1993). Also for this age group, L.J. KRIZNER and LISA SITA's *Peter Stuyvesant: New Amsterdam and the Origins of New York* (2002), illustrated with prints from the New-York Historical Society's collections, describes the contact—and clash—of cultures that occurred as the Dutch, led by their fifth and most effective governor, Peter Stuyvesant, brought strong leadership to their town. For younger readers, a more light-hearted look at New Amsterdam that nonetheless casts an appraising glance at the city's first larger-than-life politician is ARNOLD LOBEL's *On the Day Peter Stuyvesant Sailed into Town* (1971).

On the Day Peter Stuyvesant Sailed into Town, *by Arnold Lobel*

On leaving the Heye Center, cross Broadway and, turning right, walk one block along Stone Street. Now crossing Broad Street, continue on to South William, and stop at the **Dutch Revival buildings at numbers 13–15**. Built in 1903, these fanciful Dutch-gabled structures evoke the style and scale of the houses that stood on this very street centuries earlier.

A time-travel fantasy that likewise takes us back to old New Amsterdam is CAROLINE D. EMERSON's *The Magic Tunnel*, re-illustrated by JERRY ROBINSON (1964). The fun starts when two modern-day cousins, 12-year-old John and 10-year-old Sarah, find a secret spot at the front of the downtown Number 1 IRT subway. By standing in just the right place, they are magically transported to seventeenth-century lower Manhattan:

The street that led from house to house was cobbled with stones. A gutter ran down the middle of the street, and now down the gutter came a fat mother pig with five piglets. Suddenly the door of one of the little houses opened. Out came some refuse, thrown into the street. The mother pig grunted with pleasure. Then she and the little pigs began to eat noisily.

Just then Sarah noticed a windmill standing not far away. Its great arms were turning slowly . . .

—*The Magic Tunnel*

Sarah and John eventually make their way back home, but not before trying on the clothes, sampling the food, and meeting the (mostly) good people of New Amsterdam, including peg-legged Peter Stuyvesant himself.

New Amsterdam had an amazingly diverse population. As JANE MUSHABAC and ANGELA WIGAN report in their anecdote-filled chronology, *A Short and Remarkable History of New York City* (1999), by the 1640s, at least eighteen different languages were spoken there. Writing for young people in *Black Legacy: A History of New York's African Americans* (1997), WILLIAM LOREN KATZ notes that among New Amsterdam's first residents were enslaved and free African men, some of the latter of whom served the Dutch as trusted interpreters. In her picture book *The Jews of New Amsterdam* (1988), EVA DEUTSCH COSTABEL recounts the frosty reception given by Stuyvesant to the first Jewish immigrants to reach the city, via Brazil, in 1654, and their gradual acceptance as valued members of the community.

Dutch rule ended in 1664 when Governor Stuyvesant, bowing to the inevitable, surrendered New Amsterdam to a British invasion force that was determined to claim it for its king. Ever since then, the bustling port town has been called New York, after the Duke of York, brother of England's King Charles II.

Fraunces Tavern Museum

Continuing along South William Street, turn right onto narrow, cobblestone-paved Mill Lane, then right again for one block along Stone Street, then left at the pedestrian walkway in front of 85 Broad. Finally, turn left onto Pearl Street and continue to the right to **Fraunces Tavern Museum** (54 Pearl Street, southeast corner of Broad; tour information: 212-425-1778). It was here, at colonial New York's premier hostelry, built in 1719 and reconstructed between 1904 and 1907, that the revolutionary Sons of Liberty and provincial congress held some of their meetings. And it was in this tavern's Long Room, now meticulously reconstructed, that in December 1783, following the Continental army's final victory over the British, General George Washington bade his officers an emotional farewell. The adjacent museum offers changing exhibitions of art and artifacts relating to the history of colonial and early republican New York.

Washington's pivotal role as the Continental army's commander in chief is described in stirring detail in ALBERT MARRIN's *George Washington & the Founding of a Nation* (2001). The second and third volumes in a trilogy of historical novels by JAMES L. COLLIER and CHRISTOPHER COLLIER take young readers into Fraunces Tavern itself. *War Comes to Willy Freeman* (1983) tells the story of a 13-year-old African-American former slave girl, who—disguised as a boy—finds work and a temporary safe haven in the tavern's kitchen as she searches for her mother. In *Who Is Carrie?* (1984), an orphaned kitchen slave, who has long worked at the tavern, is chosen by Sam Fraunces to join the staff of President George Washington's nearby residence, where she crosses paths with Thomas Jefferson and Alexander Hamilton, among others.

On leaving Fraunces Tavern Museum, walk right on Pearl Street, pausing in Hanover Square at the statue of *Abraham de Peyster* (by George E. Bissell, 1896), a prominent merchant and early New York mayor. Continue for eight more blocks to Fulton Street. Turn right onto Fulton and continue to the area known as the **South Street Seaport Museum.** Chartered in 1967, "South Street" boasts a remarkable collection of restored nineteenth-century commercial buildings, ships, and related artifacts, including **Bowne & Co. Stationers** (211 Water Street; Mon.–Sat.: 10 A.M.–5 P.M.; 212-748-8651; www.southstseaport.org). This is a shop very much like the one where the first children's books published in New York were printed and sold.

You will find Bowne & Co. just to the left of the intersection of Fulton and Water. During the early 1800s, local printers Solomon King, Mahlon Day, and Samuel Wood all became known for the inexpensive children's books they occasionally published. Wood holds the distinction of having published the very first children's book about the city, *New-York Cries* (1808), an introduction to the city's street

New York Street Cries in Rhyme,
by Mahlon Day

merchants, complete with the peddlers' catchy sales jingles, or cries, and a miscellany of topical information.

Although the printing presses on exhibit at Bowne & Co. date from a bit later in the nineteenth century, the knowledgeable shop staff's demonstrations, in which children are encouraged to take part, give a good idea of how Wood and his rivals did their work.

You will probably want to visit some of the other exhibits and shops (including a wide selection of eateries) that comprise the museum. On coming to the end of Fulton Street, cross South Street to **Piers 16 and 17,** where the museum's collection of nineteenth- and early twentieth-century ships are permanently moored. Before leaving the piers, be sure to look out at the East River directly before you and New York Harbor to the right, and watch for a maroon-and-black Moran tugboat. One such tug inspired HARDIE GRAMATKY to create *Little Toot* (1939), his classic picture book set in these waters.

Gramatky was a 32-year-old watercolorist and *Fortune* magazine artist when he wrote and illustrated his best-known book. His studio, on Pearl Street (in a now-demolished building near the corner of Wall Street), had a view of the East River. Always plagued with poor eyesight, Gramatky would rest his eyes by looking out at the boats on the river. As he did so day after day, he became aware of a certain tugboat that always moved in lazy circles at a distance from the other tugs. From this simple observation, the story of *Little Toot* began to grow.

Little Toot,
by Hardie Gramatky

Leave South Street by retracing your steps to Fulton and Water Streets, continuing on Fulton for six blocks, to Broadway. You have now come within yards of the former site of the **World Trade Center** and of the terrorist attack that destroyed it. New Yorkers and people around the world will be struggling for years to come to terms with that terrible event and its consequences. Among the first children's books to attempt the daunting task of offering comfort and understanding are: MAIRA KALMAN's *Fireboat* (2002), a true story about the role played by a long-out-of-service fireboat in helping to extinguish the fires at Ground Zero; *New York's Bravest*, by MARY POPE OSBORNE, illustrated by STEVE JOHNSON and LOU FANCHER (2002), an original tale based on the legend of an early nineteenth-century New York fireman and folk hero named Mose Humphreys; *Chief: The Life of Peter J. Ganci,* by CHRIS GANCI (2003), a son's tribute to the Chief of the New York Fire Department, who died during the rescue effort; *Understanding September 11th,* by MITCH FRANK (2002), a *Time* reporter's distillation of the day's events; and *911-The Book of Help,* edited by MICHAEL CART (2002), a collection of reflections on the attacks by 25 writers for young people.

Our last stop takes us to a site associated with tragic events of an earlier time, the **African American Burial Ground**, located at the corner of Duane and Elk Streets. Starting from Broadway and Fulton, follow Broadway eight blocks north to Duane, turn right on Duane and continue to the end of the block. As JOYCE HANSEN and GARY McGOWAN recall in *Breaking Ground, Breaking Silence: The Story of New York's African Burial Ground* (1998), a history-making discovery occurred here in 1991, when a long-forgotten cemetery was unearthed as construction began on nearby 290 Broadway. A museum may one day rise on or near this garden lot to house the many artifacts that, as the authors explain, have given us our clearest indication of what life was like for the free and enslaved Africans living in New York City during colonial times. A sampling of artifacts is now on view during normal business hours in the lobby of 290 Broadway. Also take a moment to view Lorenzo Pace's related sculpture, *The Triumph of the Human Spirit* (1992–2000) in Federal Plaza, one block east of the Burial Ground site.

WALKING TOUR II
Immigrant New York 1

In this tour, and in the companion tour that follows, we look for evidence of the waves of immigration that shaped New York life over the last century and a half.

We begin with a trip to **Ellis Island National Monument** and the **Statue of Liberty National Monument**, both of which can be reached by ferry as part of a combined round-trip excursion from lower Manhattan's historic **Battery Park** (212-269-5755; www.statueofliberty

ferry.com) Reach the Battery Park ferry landing via the South Ferry station of the Numbers 1 and 9 trains or the nearby Bowling Green station of the Numbers 4 and 5.

From the moment of its dedication on October 28, 1886, the colossal public sculpture officially named "Liberty Enlightening the World" has stood as a universal symbol of immigrant dreams and new beginnings. Between 1892 and 1924, approximately 16 million new arrivals passed through the vast Registry Room of the federal immigrant center at **Ellis Island**, on their way to a new life. Not everyone's dreams were fulfilled there: Those showing signs of ill health or otherwise deemed "undesirable" by the authorities were returned to their homelands. Ninety-eight percent made it through.

The small library of books for young readers about these two historic sites continues to grow. For younger children, *The Story of the Statue of Liberty!*, by BETSY & GIULIO MAESTRO (1986), relates the statue's origins, planning, construction, and its meaning for the world. *Liberty!*, by ALLAN DRUMMOND (2002), describes the giant sculpture's dedication day, as experienced by a boy who participated in the ceremony. *Liberty*, by LYNN CURLEE (2000), gives a more detailed account of the artistry, engineering, and politics behind the arrival of "Lady Liberty" in New York Harbor.

Liberty!,
by Allan Drummond

I Was Dreaming to Come to America: Memories from the Ellis Island Oral History Project, selected and illustrated by VERONICA LAWLOR (1995), samples the 1,200 interviews with immigrants and immigration staff members now archived at the Ellis Island Historical Museum. ELLEN LEVINE's . . . *If Your Name Was Changed at Ellis Island*, illustrated by WAYNE PARMENTER (1993), answers frequently asked questions about immigration history and the day-to-day workings of the Ellis Island center. KAREN HESSE's moving historical novel, *Letters from Rifka* (1992), recounts the difficulties deftly overcome by a bold 12-year-old Russian Jewish girl who, in the fall of 1920, arrives at Ellis Island with a worrisome case of ringworm.

Papa wrote about Ellis Island in his letters.

He wrote that at Ellis Island you are neither in nor out of America. Ellis Island is a line separating my future from my past. Until I cross that line, I am still homeless, still an immigrant. Once I leave Ellis Island, though, I will truly be in America.
          —*Letters from Rifka*

Once you have returned via ferry to Battery Park, you may wish to visit two of the city's more recent tributes to its immigrant tradition, both of them located nearby. **The Museum of Jewish Heritage—A Living Memorial to the Holocaust** (18 First Place, Battery Park City; 212-509-6130; www.mjhnyc.org) chronicles the dynamic culture and tumultuous history of the Jewish people from the 1880s onward. To get there, simply take the footpath that leads north and west from the ferry landing and follow the signs to the museum for the equivalent of about three blocks.

Exiting the museum, walk north along the nearby riverside Esplanade. Continuing past the semicircular North Cove Yacht Harbor and glass-enclosed Winter Garden (where you may want to stop for refreshments or lunch), go on for the equivalent of one additional block until you see, on your right, the stone walls of the **Irish Hunger Memorial** (by the corner of Vesey Street and North End Avenue, Battery Park City; open all day; www.battery parkcity.org/ihm.htm). This imaginative half-acre public space, designed by Brian Tolle and dedicated in 2002, recalls the devastating blight, starting in 1845, which culminated in the starvation of one million Irish citizens and the immigration to the United States of two million more. An excellent illustrated history to read in conjunction with a visit here is SUSAN CAMPBELL BARTOLETTI's *Black Potatoes: The Story of the Great Irish Famine, 1845–1850* (2002).

We are now ready to visit the Lower East Side, located south of 14th Street and east of Broadway, a sprawling patchwork of immigrant neighborhoods, each well over a century old. Among the best introductions to this section of Manhattan, and to the immigrant experience in New York at the turn of the last century, is RUSSELL FREED-MAN'S *Immigrant Kids* (1980), illustrated with archival photographs by LEWIS W. HINE, JACOB A. RIIS, and others.

You may wish to tailor this ambitious walking tour to suit your interests and stamina. We begin at the intersection of Kenmare and Mulberry Streets, which can be reached by taking the J or M train to the Bowery station and walking three blocks west on Kenmare.

Set around 1890, primarily along the stretch of Mulberry Street between Kenmare and Canal Streets that still constitutes the heart of **Little Italy**, *Peppe the Lamplighter*, by ELISA BARTONE, illustrated by TED LEWIN (1993), recalls a bittersweet side of immigrant life. In this story based on the author's own family recollections, a poor widowed Italian father of nine feels torn when, to help out, his young son takes a job as a lamplighter—menial work that the father considers beneath his family's dignity. As you continue south along Mul-

Peppe the Lamplighter, by Elisa Bartone, *illustrated by Ted Lewin*

berry, look for tenement-style buildings like those depicted in Lewin's well-researched watercolors.

STEVEN KROLL's novel, *Sweet America: An Immigrant's Story* (2000), recounts the trials and triumphs of a 14-year-old Italian immigrant newspaper boy also living on Mulberry Street during the 1880s.

Now cross Canal Street and enter central **Chinatown**. A small Chinese community had already taken root in lower Manhattan by the 1850s, but the nation's highly restrictive immigration laws kept a tight rein on Chinatown's growth until 1965.

The best way to experience Chinatown is simply to wander its narrow, bustling streets on your own—preferably with a reliable restaurant guide at the ready! As you do so, however, look for shops and street scenes like those depicted in two picture books—one written in verse, the other in prose—that offer impressionistic, first-person portraits of the neighborhood: *My Chinatown: One Year in Poems*, by KAM MAK (2001), and *Chinatown*, by WILLIAM LOW (1997). *Lion Dancer: Ernie Wan's Chinese New Year*, by KATE WATERS and MADELINE SLOVENZ-LOW, photographed by MARTHA COOPER (1990), documents an important event in one young neighborhood resident's life: Ernie Wan's first performance in the traditional Lion Dance, staged annually in the streets of Chinatown in celebration of Chinese New Year.

Chinatown,
by William Low

Those interested in learning more about the history and cultural background of the Chinese immigrant population living in New York and beyond will want to visit **The Museum of Chinese in the Americas** (70 Mulberry Street, 2nd floor, corner of Bayard; Tues.–Sat.: 12–5 P.M; 212-619-4785; www.moca-nyc.org).

Leave Chinatown by walking south on Mott Street and turning left onto Pell. Halfway along this short street, turn right onto zigzagging Doyers, and follow it across The Bowery to Division Street. Walk one long block along Division and, passing under the Manhattan Bridge, turn left onto Eldridge Street. You have now entered what was once the heart of the Jewish Lower East Side.

Pause to notice **17 Eldridge Street**, home of the young heroine of ELSA OKON RAEL's picture book *When Zaydeh Danced on Eldridge Street* (1997), illustrated by MARJORIE PRICEMAN. Just across from this tenement building, at **numbers 12–16**, is **K'Hal Adath Jeshurun** (popularly known as the **Eldridge Street Synagogue**), where the sprightly Zeesie and her usually severe *zaydeh* (Yiddish for "grandfather") together dance the night away in celebration of the joyful Jewish holiday of Simchas Torah. Built in 1887, this synagogue (now lovingly restored) ranked among the neighborhood's busiest Jewish houses of worship around the turn of the century. For tour information, contact the Lower East Side Conservancy (212-585-1200; e-mail LESConservancy@aol.com).

When Zaydeh Danced on Eldridge Street,
by Elsa Okon Rael,
illustrated by Marjorie Priceman

Walk one block north on Eldridge, turning right onto Canal and continuing for four blocks to Essex Street, to find more evidence of this neighborhood's Jewish community. This is a good place to recall the classic fictional account of New York Jewish immigrant life, SYDNEY TAYLOR's *All-of-a-Kind Family*, illustrated by HELEN JOHN (1951). A sort of Lower East Side *Little Women*, this episodic novel

K'Hal Adath Jeshurun
(Eldridge Street Synagogue)

Essex Street, between East Broadway and Hester Street

set in the year 1912 dramatizes the everyday routines and holiday rituals of a first-generation American Jewish family with five daughters ranging in age from 4 to 10. Taylor based her first novel and its four sequels on memories of growing up on the Lower East Side and later in the Bronx. She modeled Sarah, the middle child, on herself.

Because their papa owns a junk shop, these five girls live in somewhat better circumstances than do most of their Lower East Side neighbors. Home for them (the author never specifies the address) is a four-room, floor-through apartment in a two-story private house, not one of the area's typically cramped and poorly ventilated tenement flats. Nonetheless, the sisters take care to watch their pennies. As Taylor, looking wistfully back from the vantage point of the more settled and prosperous 1950s, reminds readers:

Almost no East Side child owned a book when Mamma's children were little girls. That was an unheard-of luxury. It was heavenly enough to be able to borrow books from the public library and that was where the children always went on Friday afternoons. Right after school, they rushed off happily to get fresh reading material for the week end. Even Gertie who was not yet old enough to "belong" took the weekly trip to look at the picture magazines.

—*All-of-a-Kind Family*

Although Taylor does not identify it by name, the library frequented by the girls in *All-of-a-Kind Family* is certainly the New

Seward Park branch of the New York Public Library

York Public's **Seward Park branch** (192 East Broadway). If you wish to have a look at this historic building, walk one block east from the corner of Essex and Canal; the library stands on the far side of Seward Park.

During the early years of the last century, the Seward Park branch became legendary for its exceptionally long hours of operation and its correspondingly heavy use by immigrant patrons eager to learn English and to better themselves.

Lower East Side Tenement Museum (center)

Returning to the corner of Essex and Canal, walk north on Essex for two blocks. Then, turning left onto Grand, continue for two blocks and then turn right onto Orchard Street. Walk one more block to the **Lower East Side Tenement Museum**, 97 Orchard Street (Visitors' Center at 90 Orchard Street; reservations necessary: 212-431-0233; www.tenement. org). This unusual museum occupies a five-story, ten-flat tenement building typical of the neighborhood. From 1863 (the year it was built) to 1935 (when it was boarded up), this one structure was home to an incredible seven thousand immigrants from Germany, Ireland, Italy, and eastern Europe. The building has been restored as a kind of time capsule depicting the living quarters and conditions of particular resident families from different periods in the building's eventful past.

Linda Granfield's *97 Orchard Street, New York*, photographed by Arlene Alda (2001), is a young reader's introduction to the museum—a landmark structure preserved not for its architectural uniqueness or beauty, but as a record of the sometimes shocking conditions that so many of our immigrant ancestors were forced to endure. A more detailed account of tenement life, with color photos of 97 Orchard Street's interiors, is found in *Tenement*, by Raymond Bial (2002).

On leaving the museum, walk north one block to the corner of Orchard and Delancey Streets and the approximate setting of ELSA OKON RAEL's *What Zeesie Saw on Delancey Street*, illustrated by MARJORIE PRICEMAN (1996). This picture book recalls the eastern Jewish immigrant community's custom of periodically gathering for a party, the highlight of which was an auction of home-cooked delicacies. The money thus raised would be used to bankroll friends' and relatives' passage from the Old Country or for some other worthy purpose. On the evening in question, adventurous Zeesie wanders away from the main party and has an eye-opening adventure that teaches her an important lesson about the rewards of charitable giving.

More Lower Manhattan Books

Dreams of the Golden Country: The Diary of Ziporah Feldman, a Jewish Immigrant Girl, New York City, 1903, by KATHRYN LASKY (1998). A skillful fictionalized first-person account of Jewish immigrant life on the Lower East Side.

Happy Birthday Mr. Kang, by SUSAN L. ROTH (2001). Mr. Kang, a Chinese immigrant, makes a new life for himself in New York's Chinatown, which includes a Sunday morning ritual that reminds him of his old home.

The Wigwam and the Longhouse, by CHARLOTTE and DAVID YUE (2000). A detailed description of the daily lives and living conditions, in precolonial times, of eastern North America's woodland native peoples, including those who inhabited present-day New York City.

GREENWICH VILLAGE ▪ THE EAST VILLAGE ▪ SOHO

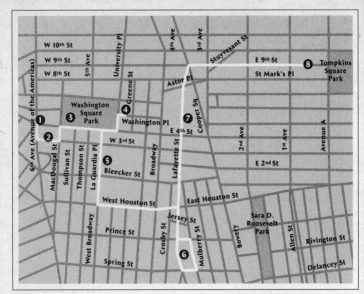

▲ Walking Tour I

❶ W. 4th St. Courts

❷ George Stable's block

❸ Washington Square Park

❹ Triangle Shirtwaist Factory

❺ Mayor Fiorello H. La Guardia sculpture

❻ Madlenka's block

❼ Astor Library (425 Lafayette St.)

❽ E. 9th St. between 1st Ave. and Ave. A
(inspiration for *The Gardener*)

▼ Walking Tour II

1 7th Ave. & W. 14th St.

2 Walter Brooks house (27 Bank St.)

3 69 Bank St. (former Bank Street College of Education)

4 Robert McCloskey studio (280 W. 12th St.)

5 Maurice Sendak apt. (92 Charles St.)

6 Cobble Court (121 Charles St.)

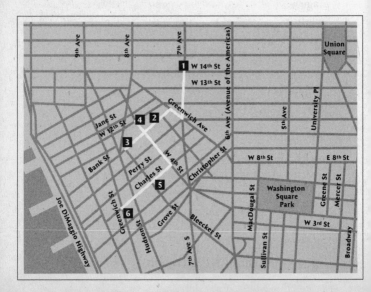

GREENWICH VILLAGE

■

THE EAST VILLAGE

■

SOHO

*O*n 1819, the year that Herman Melville was born on Pearl Street near the southern tip of Manhattan, Greenwich Village—located west of Fifth Avenue, between West 14th and West Houston Streets—was still a bucolic suburb, a fresh-air haven for New Yorkers eager to escape the city's summertime cholera and yellow fever epidemics. By the mid-1820s, however, the first of several waves of development began to transform the area, with construction of fashionable homes followed by the addition of churches, schools, shops, theaters, and parks. Preservation-minded early nineteenth-century Villagers fought to save their colonial-era winding streets at a time when much of Manhattan was being mapped out in a uniform grid. By the early 1900s, the neighborhood's eccentric backwater ambience (and cheap rents, as moneyed New Yorkers moved inexorably northward) made the Village a desirable home for artists, writers, musicians, revolutionaries, and other people with idealistic goals and new ideas.

WALKING TOUR I

We start our tour at the corner of West 4th Street and Avenue of the Americas (West 4th Street station of the A, C, E, F, and Q lines). From June to August, the **West 4th Street Courts** (east side of Avenue of the Americas) is home to some of the best amateur basketball anywhere. Photographer and poet CHARLES R. SMITH JR. captures the action here (and at other street courts around town) in his picture book *Rimshots* (1999).

Rimshots,
by Charles R. Smith Jr.

Now walk east one block from West 3rd Street and Avenue of the Americas to MacDougal Street, the block where 12-year-old George Stable, hero of *The Teddy Bear Habit*, by JAMES LINCOLN COLLIER (1967), lives with his graphic-artist father. George is a gifted musician with professional aspirations—and a paralyzing case of stage fright that he's able to overcome only by taking a cherished childhood toy bear along with him to auditions. As the story unfolds, he innocently gets caught up in a mystery involving a theft and a rather surly village character. In the course of disentangling himself from the mess, George finds the courage he needs.

After taking in the still vaguely bohemian MacDougal Street scene that is *The Teddy Bear Habit*'s backdrop, walk north one block along MacDougal to **Washington**

Bein' with You This Way, by W. Nikola-Lisa,
illustrated by Michael Bryant

Square Park. Enter the park, for decades a world crossroads of youth culture and the setting of W. NIKOLA-LISA's sprightly read-aloud picture book, *Bein' with You This Way*, illustrated by MICHAEL BRYANT (1994). If you look closely at the energetic watercolors, you will glimpse several park features of interest to children: the chess tables (made famous by the film *Searching for Bobby*

Fischer) at the southwest entrance, the nearby asphalt mounds for skateboarders, and a perennial complement of New York pigeons.

The Park Book, *by Charlotte Zolotow, illustrated by H. A. Rey*

The Park Book (1944), the first picture book written by CHARLOTTE ZOLO-TOW and one of the first American titles illustrated by H.A. REY, chronicles a day in the life of Washington Square Park. At the time of their collaboration, Zolotow and Rey both lived in the neighborhood.

Exit Washington Square Park to the east by the path leading past the statue of nineteenth-century Italian pa-

More Village ▪ SoHo Artists and Writers Over the Years

MARCIA BROWN • ERIC CARLE • REMY CHARLIP • LEE BENNETT HOPKINS • ROBERT LAWSON • MUNRO LEAF • ANITA LOBEL • ANN M. MARTIN • EVE MERRIAM • URSULA NORDSTROM • PEGGY PARISH • URI SHULEVITZ • WILLIAM STEIG • MARK TWAIN • TOMI UNGERER • LEONARD WEISGARD • E.B. WHITE • VERA B. WILLIAMS • DIANE WOLKSTEIN • JANE YOLEN

triot Giuseppe Garibaldi. Crossing Washington Square East, walk one block east along the north side of Washington Place, pausing just before Greene Street to read the two plaques on New York University's Brown Building, which once housed the **Triangle Shirtwaist Factory**. Here, on March 25, 1911, a horrific fire resulted in the deaths of 146 young women factory workers, most of whom had not been provided with any emergency escape route. In the aftermath of the tragedy, workers' rights received heightened attention, and emerging labor unions found a renewed sense of purpose. Books for young readers that best relate the story of this harrowing episode in our nation's history include *Fire at the Triangle Factory*, by HOLLY LITTLEFIELD, illustrated by MARY O'KEEFE YOUNG (1996); *Ashes of Roses*, by MARY JANE AUCH (2002), a novel centering on the experiences of a group of Irish immigrant working girls; and (though not written expressly for young people) RUTH DAIGON's *Payday at the Triangle* (2001), a moving collection of first-person verse monologues, cast in the voices of witnesses to the tragedy and of the workers themselves.

Fiorello H. La Guardia,
by Neil Estern

Returning to Washington Square East, proceed to the southeast corner of the park, turn right and walk one block along Washington Square South. Then turn left onto La Guardia Place, continuing for a block and a half until you come to the sculpture of the jaunty man for whom the street is named, **Mayor Fiorello H. La Guardia.** A dynamic social reformer and inspiring popular leader, La Guardia was also a showman who loved to be heard. During a 1945 newspaper deliveryman strike, he made sure that the city's children kept up with the comics by going on the radio and reading *Dick Tracy.* GLORIA KAMEN tells the story of this irrepressible New Yorker in *Fiorello: His Honor, the Little Flower* (1981).

Continue south to the end of La Guardia Place and cross busy West Houston Street, the dividing line between the Village and SoHo. Walk east six blocks to the intersection of East Houston and Lafayette Street. Turn right onto Lafayette, walking one block to Prince Street. The city block defined by the stretch of Prince Street immediately to your left, of Lafayette just ahead (to the south), and the connecting blocks of Spring and

Mulberry Streets, comprise the setting of PETER SÍS's fantasy-laden picture-book tribute to melting-pot New York, *Madlenka* (2000).

Some New York neighborhood shops take root and become permanent fixtures while others come and go. *Madlenka*'s readers will want to make the complete circuit of the young heroine's route to see how many of her shopkeeper friends are still in business.

Madlenka,
by Peter Sís

Return to Lafayette Street and follow it north for four longish blocks, either on foot or by bus. This broad thoroughfare, which extends from Park Row by City Hall north to Astor Place, pays homage to the Marquis de Lafayette, the French soldier-statesman who came to the aid of the American colonists during our nation's war for independence from Britain. The street was newly laid out following Lafayette's triumphal 1824–1825 return visit to the city. JEAN FRITZ's pithy chapter-book biography, *Why Not, Lafayette?*, illustrated by RONALD HIMLER (1999), tells the inspiring tale of this life bravely lived.

Crossing East 4th Street and continuing one more block north along Lafayette, notice on the right the magnificent former **Astor Library** building at **number 425**, now the **Public Theater**. Free library service in New York began here in 1854—although not for children, who had to wait another fifty years. In 1895 the Astor Library merged with the Lenox Library and the Tilden Trust to form the central branch of the New York Public Library, at 42nd Street and Fifth Avenue [see pages 41–45].

Public Theater,
formerly the Astor Library

Continue north along Lafayette,

turning right onto East 9th Street, and follow East 9th until you reach the block between First Avenue and Avenue A. It was here that DAVID SMALL made many of his sketches for *The Gardener* (1997), a picture book written by his wife, SARAH STEWART. *The Gardener* tells the

The Gardener, *by Sarah Stewart, illustrated by David Small*

Depression-era story of a generous-hearted, resourceful farm girl's first visit to the big city. By wielding her green thumb in and around her uncle Jim's bakery, Lydia Grace brings a bit of the country—and hope—into the older person's hardscrabble tenement life. Small based the kitchen in Uncle Jim's apartment on the restored Baldizzi family kitchen, dating from 1935, on view at the Lower East Side Tenement Museum [see page 16]. (The vast, skylit train terminal that serves as Lydia Grace's point of entry to New York is Manhattan's original Pennsylvania Station. Sadly, this great building was demolished in 1965 to make way for Madison Square Garden.)

WALKING TOUR II

This tour highlights a few of the many Greenwich Village houses and haunts where children's-book authors and illustrators have lived and worked. Start at the southwest corner of 7th Avenue and West 14th Street and walk south three blocks, turning right onto Greenwich Avenue (a shop-lined street that slices diagonally through this part of town). Cross Greenwich and follow it for one block to Bank Street. Continue along Bank Street to the town house at **number 27** (now divided into apartments) where WALTER R. BROOKS wrote most of the **Freddy the Pig** books.

Brooks also wrote for *The New Yorker* and in 1931 produced a travel book, *New York: An Intimate Guide*, in which he downplayed his neighborhood's reputation as an enclave of wild-eyed bohemians. "The sincere artist seldom has time to grow a beard or follow the rigid rules of the unconventional," Brooks, who favored tweeds and wing tips, observed. ". . . You may live [in the Village] for weeks and not see a single fake artist—and if you see a real one, you won't know it."

69 Bank Street, first home of the Bank Street College of Education

Continue one more block along Bank Street to **number 69.** This building, a one-time yeast factory and now a luxury condominium, served as the headquarters of the Bureau of Educational Experiments (later called the **Bank Street College of Education**) from 1930 to 1969. It was here, under the direction of founder Lucy Sprague Mitchell, that groundbreaking research in early childhood development was carried out, that many of America's first preschool teachers received their training, and that pioneering writers for the very young—notably Margaret Wise Brown and Ruth Krauss—learned their craft [see page 83].

Backtrack half a block on Bank Street and turn left onto West 4th Street, continuing one block to where it intersects West 12th Street. (Such seemingly illogical, Mad Hatterish crisscrossings of numbered streets are all part of the Village's legendary charm!) Crossing West 4th, walk a few steps to the right along West 12th, stopping in front of **280 West 12th Street**, the row house where Robert McCloskey created the art for *Make Way for Ducklings*. In 1939, McCloskey moved to New York from Boston, where he had already made numerous sketches of the Public Garden, State House, and other landmarks featured in that most quintessentially Boston of all picture books. It was in New York, however, that he found the models for his ducklings. When not drawing preserved specimens at the American Museum of Natural History [see pages 79–82], McCloskey sketched the

Long Island ducklings—as many as twelve at a time—that he purchased at a local market and kept in his rented fourth-floor studio. The bathtub served as a makeshift pond. McCloskey shared the West 12th Street studio with another future Caldecott Medal winner, **Marc Simont**, who, as a favor to his friend, would hold a duckling in a needed pose while McCloskey sketched.

Turning left onto West 4th Street, walk four blocks to Charles Street and turn right onto Charles, stopping at **number 92**, where MAURICE SENDAK lived while writing and illustrating *The Sign on Rosie's Door* and drawing the illustrations for ELSE HOLMELUND MINARIK's *Little Bear* and numerous other early works. (Sendak later moved a few blocks to the west, to an apartment at **29 West 9th Street**, where he created *Where the Wild Things Are*.)

Proceed west on Charles, crossing Bleecker and Hudson Streets. A few steps farther bring you to the white dollhouselike clapboard cottage at **121 Charles Street**. This wonderland dwelling, known as **Cobble Court** for the stones set in the front yard, was *Goodnight Moon* author MARGARET WISE BROWN's writing studio and sometime home from 1943 to 1952. When Brown occupied the eighteenth-century farmhouse, it was located elsewhere—at 1835 York Avenue and East 71st Street. Hidden from view by a tenement row, the house was reached via a ground-floor passageway through one of the tenements. The glamorous author decked out her tiny sitting room with fur-upholstered furniture. A fireplace was the only heat source. GARTH WILLIAMS depicted the fanciful house in his illustrations for Brown's Little Golden Book, *Mister Dog*. Artist *Clement Hurd* was a guest there when Brown first showed him the manuscript of *Goodnight Moon*. Threatened with demolition, Cobble Court was moved to its present location in 1967.

More Greenwich Village ∎
East Village ∎ SoHo Books

Diary of a Little Girl in Old New York, by CATHERINE E. HAVENS (2001). This authentic diary for the years 1849–1850 describes the life of a 10-year-old whose family lived somewhere along fashionable Ninth Street between Sixth Avenue and Broadway.

The Invisible Day, by MARTHE JOCELYN, illustrated by ABBY CARTER (1997). The first of a series of comic novels about the Stoner family, SoHo residents whose 10-year-old daughter, Billie, finds a way to make herself invisible.

Jenny and the Cat Club, by ESTHER AVERILL (2003). Here reprinted in one volume are five complete storybooks about the Cat Club, that redoubtable band of Village felines whose personal foibles and social dilemmas bear an uncanny resemblance to our own.

The Two Reds, by WILLIAM LIPKIND, illustrated by NICOLAS MORDVINOFF (1950). Red the boy and Red the cat both live in the East Village, where the streets are riotously noisy and the backyards serenely quiet, and just about every place seems worth exploring.

The Other Shepards, by ADELE GRIFFIN (1998). Holland Shepard and her younger sister, Geneva, grow up in the shadow of three siblings who died in a car crash long before they were born. The West Village home where they gradually come to terms with their ghostly legacy is the pre–Civil War row house at **176 Waverly Place,** between Christopher and West 10th Streets.

FLATIRON DISTRICT ▪ GRAMERCY PARK ▪ CHELSEA

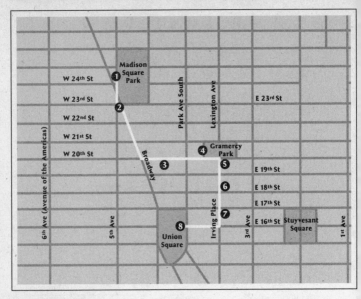

▲ Walking Tour I

1. W. 24th St. & Broadway / Fifth Ave.
2. Flatiron Building
3. Theodore Roosevelt Birthplace
4. Gramercy Park
5. Hotel Irving / Irving House
6. Pete's Tavern
7. Washington Irving House (122 E.17th St.)
8. Union Square

▼ Walking Tour II

1. 8th Ave. & W. 23rd St.
2. Chelsea House (420 W. 23rd St.)
3. Clement Moore–style rowhouses (428 – 446 & 450 W. 23rd St.)
4. Clement Clarke Moore Park
5. General Theological Seminary

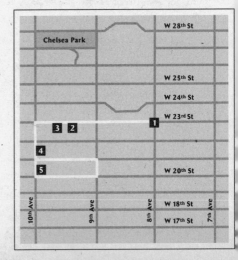

THE FLATIRON DISTRICT

■

GRAMERCY PARK

■

CHELSEA

*T*he Flatiron District takes its name from one of the city's most flamboyant structures. Built in 1903, the **Flatiron Building**, at 175 Fifth Avenue, was among the city's first skyscrapers, and it has always held a special place in New Yorkers' imaginations. Onlookers have compared its striking triangular wedge shape to a slice of pie and the prow of a mysteriously landlocked ship. But it was the building's likeness to a tailor's iron that set the popular designation for an office tower officially named the Fuller Building by its original owner.

Dreams of the Rarebit Fiend,
by Winsor McCay

WALKING TOUR I

We begin this tour by having a look at this New York landmark from the small triangular traffic island located at the intersection where West 24th Street crosses both Broadway and Fifth Avenue (23rd Street station, N and R lines).

When new, the Flatiron Building occupied a prime location in New York's central entertainment district, home to expensive restaurants, opulent theaters, and fashionable hotels. No wonder that when artist WINSOR MCCAY wanted to depict New York's architectural highspots in his proto-surrealist comic strip *Dreams of the Rarebit Fiend*, he chose to include the Flatiron Building along with the Statue of Liberty and the Brooklyn Bridge. ROXIE MUNRO captures with precision the strangeness and grandeur of this building in *The Inside-Outside Book of New York City* (2001), a visual tour book that

The Inside-Outside Book of New York City,
by Roxie Munro

shows the view looking out from the Flatiron Building and other city landmarks as well as the view from the street.

Walk southeast along Broadway, stopping if you like to explore Madison Square—a park named for the nation's fourth president—and cross East 23rd Street, walking past the Flatiron Building and onto East 20th Street. Turn left and continue to 28 East 20th Street, the **Theodore Roosevelt Birthplace National Historic Site** (Mon.–Fri.: 9 A.M.– 5 P.M.; 212-260-1616; www.nps.gov/thrb).

In fact, the luxurious private home in which the twenty-sixth president spent his childhood no longer exists. The Roosevelts' house occupied the present site of the adjoining museum. The brownstone open to the public for tours is a period twin that has been re-

Theodore Roosevelt Birthplace National Historic Site

stored and furnished to evoke the spirit of the original 1848 Roosevelt town house.

Heir to a socially prominent New York merchant family, young "Teedie" lived a life of privilege marred by frail health. Just beyond the third-floor nursery, visitors will find a porch like the one where father Theodore, Sr., installed a well-equipped gymnasium for the benefit of his asthmatic son. The story of this extraordinary American who went on to lead cavalry charges, create the National Parks system, win the Nobel Peace Prize, and write more than forty books is ably retold by JEAN FRITZ in *Bully for You, Teddy Roosevelt!*, illustrated by MIKE WIMMER (1991).

Walk east along East 20th Street, crossing Park Avenue South and continuing another half block until you reach the southwest corner of **Gramercy Park.**

This elegant green space and the well-preserved nineteenth-century buildings that frame it offer a rare, largely intact glimpse of New York's Victorian past. In keeping with the neighborhood's reputation as an exclusive preserve, the park remains closed to the public. Only residents of adjoining properties have keys to the gates.

One such lucky New Yorker was LUDWIG BEMELMANS [see p. 62], who lived at the **Hotel Irving**, 26 Gramercy Park South (now **Irving House**, an apartment building), in the late 1930s, while creating *Madeline* (1939). Although set in Paris, Bemelmans's best-loved tale was inspired in part by one of Gramercy Park's more colorful residents. Henriette Desportes had moved from Paris to New York circa 1850 following her acquittal on charges of conspiring with a French duke to murder the latter's wife. In her new life, the beautiful Frenchwoman taught school in Gramercy Park to thirteen small girls. The muffed and bonneted youngsters' daily constitutional—six times around the park in rows of two—soon became a well-known neighborhood ritual. Newbery Medal winner (and grandniece of Henriette) RACHEL FIELD described the procession in her 1938 novel for adults, *All This, and Heaven Too*. The demure Miss Clavel of *Madeline* fame is, however, a far cry from her notorious real-life inspiration.

Fourteen-year-old Davey Mitchell, the hero of EMILY NEVILLE's Newbery Medal–winning *It's Like This, Cat* (1963), lives in an apartment around the corner from the park on Third Avenue. Davey's father, a successful lawyer, and his self-absorbed, neurotic mom, have little time for their son. Freely moving about the city by subway and on foot, Davey gathers around him an unlikely assortment of friends, all loners and individualists like himself. His adventures take him all around town, from the beach at Brooklyn's Coney Island to Inwood Park (at the northern tip of Manhattan), and to the Winter Garden Theater (1634 Broadway at West 51st Street), where Davey attends a matinee performance of the original cast production of *West Side Story.*

From Gramercy Park South, turn south (by the center gate) onto Irving Place, a street named for famed nineteeth-century New York writer WASHINGTON IRVING. Continue to **Pete's Tavern** (formerly Healy's Café), 129 East 18th Street (northeast corner of Irving Place). This restaurant/bar dating from 1829 was a favorite of WILLIAM SYDNEY PORTER, the short-story writer known as O. HENRY, who penned his widely anthologized Christmas fable, "The Gift of the Magi," in the second booth on the right past the entrance. A good young people's collection in which to find this classic tale is *The Gift of the Magi and Other Stories*, by O. Henry, illustrated by MICHAEL DOOLING (1997). Nearly forty years later, Ludwig Bemelmans wrote *Madeline* at Pete's (though no one recalls just where he was sitting!). A plaque to the left of the entrance commemorates both O. Henry's and Bemelmans's association with this Gramercy Park institution.

Continue south on Irving Place, pausing at the southwest corner of Irving and East 17th Street to notice the four-story brick house (**122 East 17th Street**) where Washington Irving lived. Be sure also to look directly across Irving Place at the large bust of America's first notable literary writer, which stands in front of the high school named for him. A satirical essayist, fiction writer, and biographer, Irving is best remembered today for two beguiling short stories rooted in folkloric tradition, "Rip Van Winkle" and "The Legend of Sleepy Hollow." These tales, both set in the Hudson Valley north of the city, have been retold in a pair of picture books with somewhat simplified language by contemporary "primitive" artist WILL MOSES, great-grandson of Grandma Moses.

Continuing south along Irving Place, turn right onto East 16th Street, walk one block, and cross Park Avenue South. Enter and take the time to explore **Union Square,** with its playgrounds, spectacular farmers' market (Mon., Wed., Fri., Sat.: 8 A.M.–6 P.M.), and sculptures of George Washington, the Marquis de Lafayette, Mahatma Gandhi, and Abraham Lincoln. Ragged Dick, the plucky title character of rags-to-riches author HO-RATIO ALGER, JR.'s, first novel (1867), has this to say about the fourteen-and-a-half-foot-tall equestrian statue of Washington in this park:

Washington,
by Henry Kirke Brown

He's growed some since he was President. If he'd been as tall as that when he fit in the Revolution, he'd have walloped the British some, I reckon.
                                                            —*Ragged Dick*

The Pushcart War, *by Jean Merrill, illustrated by Ronni Solbert*

From the Civil War era onward, Union Square has been the site of political rallies, protest demonstrations, and public vigils. Novelist JEAN MERRILL and illustrator RONNI SOLBERT recall this aspect of the park's historic legacy in *The Pushcart War* (1964), a mordantly witty mock-documentary account of a rapidly escalating turf war between New York's truck drivers and the city's remaining street peddlers. The action in this David and Goliath satire about the perils of unchecked commercial expansion ranges widely around Manhattan, from the Plaza Hotel to the Lower East Side's Delancey Street. In one pivotal scene, New York Mayor Emmet P. Cudd speaks out in defense of the truckers at an election rally held in Union Square. Building his case on a single (and rather preposterous) example, the mayor argues that the more peanut butter is trucked through New York, the better it will be for the city's economy. More peanut butter, he concludes, inevitably means more and bigger trucks. It all sounds a bit forced and more than a little nutty.

A picture book that summons up the helter-skelter atmosphere in and around the park during the 1930s (including the neighborhood's long-demolished Third Avenue elevated train station), is *New Yorker* artist EDWARD SOREL's *The Saturday Kid*, co-authored by CHERYL CARLESIMO (2000). Based on memories of his own New York childhood, Sorel describes the giddy sensation of looking out from the front window of the speeding El and imagining himself, Walter Mitty-style, piloting an airplane.

Read All About Them: The Sculptures of Union Square Park

Gandhi, by DEMI (2001). This picture-book biography, with elegant, Buddhist-inspired art, traces Gandhi's growth from shy child to spiritual and political leader.

Gandhi: Beautiful Soul, by JOHN B. SEVERANCE (1997). For older readers, a thoroughly researched account of Gandhi's life and philosophy, illustrated with archival photographs.

George Washington & the Founding of a Nation, by ALBERT MARRIN (2001). A full-dress biography of the Father of Our Country, with detailed discussions of his military career and presidency as well as of the boy and man behind the myth.

Lincoln: A Photobiography, by RUSSELL FREEDMAN (1987). This Newbery winner humanizes the great man against the backdrop of one of American history's most turbulent times.

Why Not, Lafayette?, by JEAN FRITZ; illustrated by RONALD HIMLER (1999). The French soldier and statesman whom George Washington treated like a son emerges in this concise biography as a fearless and level-headed idealist.

WALKING TOUR II

In Search of "A Visit from St. Nicholas"

Bits and pieces of the old New York of CLEMENT CLARKE MOORE, the man usually credited with having composed America's iconic Christmas poem, can be glimpsed along the streets of Chelsea, the neighborhood between 14th and 28th Streets extending from Seventh Avenue west to the Hudson River.

Moore belonged to one of New York City's most

prominent families. His father served as Episcopal bishop of the Diocese of New York for thirty-five years. Moore himself was a professor of ancient languages as well as an entrepreneur who during the late 1820s oversaw the transformation of his family's rural estate, Chelsea, into an upscale residential row-house neighborhood.

According to legend, Clement Moore was returning home by horse-drawn sleigh from lower Manhattan on the evening of December 24, 1822, when the words of the poem beginning " 'Twas the night before Christmas . . ." first stirred—visions of sugarplums and all—in his head. Later that evening, at home, Moore wrote down the poem as a gift for his three daughters. The following year, he allowed his rhyme to be published anonymously in a Troy, New York, newspaper (gentlemen did not admit to writing for newspapers in those days). In 1844, as the fame of the oft-reprinted holiday poem continued to grow, he finally claimed authorship. (A literary scholar-detective has in recent years laid out a provocative, if inconclusive, case for Poughkeepsie gentleman-poet Henry Livingston, Jr., as the true author of the celebrated rhyme. In this colorful scenario, the famously grinchlike Moore emerges as an opportunist, liar, and literary thief!)

Prior to the 1820s, most New Yorkers regarded either New Year's Day or St. Nicholas Day (December 6), rather than Christmas, as their major winter holiday. Enthusiasm for the poem helped to set not only our modern American tradition of Christmas celebration but also the now familiar image of St. Nick—Santa Claus—as a plump and jovial deliveryman extraordinaire.

Our tour begins on the southwest corner of Eighth Avenue and West 23rd Street (West 23rd Street station of the C and E subway lines). Walk west, crossing Ninth Avenue, and stop at **number 420** to read the plaque marking the approximate site of **Chelsea House**, the Moore family home. The elegant row houses (originally one-family dwellings, now apartments) along this block, at **numbers 428–446** and **450**, epitomize the high-end style of development for which Moore was known.

Continue west along West 23rd Street, turning left

onto Tenth Avenue. Walk a block and a half to the entrance to **Clement Clarke Moore Park** (1968). You will want to read the two commemorative plaques by the entrance gate. This unassuming urban oasis, with its playground, shade trees, and benches, makes a good resting spot. When you are ready to leave, turn left at the gate, continuing along Tenth Avenue to the corner of West 20th Street. The cluster of imposing Gothic Revival–style buildings you see beside you comprise the **General Theological Seminary**,

General Theological Seminary

for which Clement Moore donated the land and where he taught. As you walk along West 20th Street toward Ninth Avenue, gaze in at this sprawling, cloisterlike compound, built on the site of a Moore family apple orchard.

Numerous picture-book editions of "An Account of a Visit from St. Nicholas" have appeared over the years. Among those worth finding are: *The Night Before Christmas*, with BRUCE WHATLEY's dazzlingly rendered paintings (1999); *The Night Before Christmas*, featuring posed sepia-tone photographs by RAQUEL JARAMILLO (2001); and *The New Yorker* cartoonist JOHN O'BRIEN's witty *The Night Before Christmas Coloring Book* (1981). With a nod to the growing controversy over the poem's authorship, illustrator MATT TAVARES, in his visually striking *'Twas the Night Before Christmas* (2002), attributes the text to "Anonymous."

MIDTOWN MANHATTAN

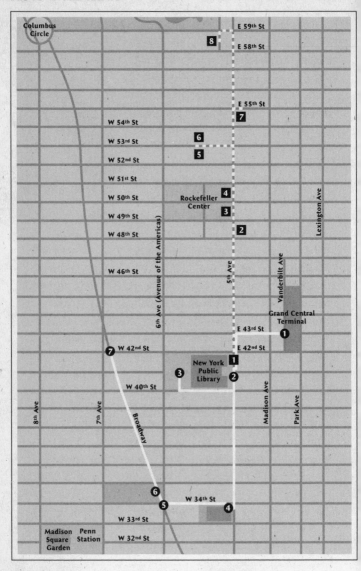

Walking Tour I

1. Grand Central Terminal / Metropolitan Life Insurance Co.
2. The New York Public Library
3. Bryant Park
4. Empire State Building
5. Herald Square
6. Macy's
7. Times Square

Walking Tour II - - -

1. The New York Public Library (42nd St. & 5th Ave.)
2. Charles Scribner's Sons
3. Rockefeller Center Promenade
4. Atlas
5. Donnell Library Center / Central Children's Room
6. Museum of Modern Art
7. St. Regis Hotel / King Cole Lounge
8. The Plaza Hotel / Palm Court

MIDTOWN
MANHATTAN

"It's not called grand for nothing!"

—*Next Stop Grand Central*, by MAIRA KALMAN

The next we knew it was morning and the conductor was hollering: "G-rand Central Station!" "Does he mean it's New York?" I says to Perry, and we asked him, and he says "Where else?"

Well, we went walking around the streets looking up at the high buildings till our necks ached, and that darn suitcase weighing like a grand piano. We were sort of bewildered, I guess. We'd never seen so many people in our lives and we'd never heard such noise. "I wish I'd gone to an orphan asylum instead," I says, just about ready to cry. But Perry got mad. "I think it's swell," he says. "I'm going to live here forever." The funny thing is that Perry's married now, and running a poultry farm in Jersey; and here I am still in the city, and crazy about it.

—Miss Pearl, the hairdresser, recalling her arrival in New York, in *The Saturdays*, by ELIZABETH ENRIGHT

We begin our tour of midtown Manhattan with a landmark that has long served as one of the city's gateways: **Grand Central Terminal** (East 42nd Street between Vanderbilt and Park Avenues).

The best way to approach this splendid structure is by foot. Enter at the corner of 42nd and Vanderbilt and follow the signs (and crowds) to the Main Concourse. You are now standing in one of New York's most magnificent public spaces—and one of the city's best places for people watching, a fact celebrated in **Next Stop Grand Central**, by MAIRA KALMAN (1999).

In 1998, Grand Central underwent a major renova-

Next Stop Grand Central, *by Maira Kalman*

tion. Because the vital commuter hub had to remain open throughout the overhaul, artists were commissioned to create temporary murals to conceal the work. Among the outsized, smile-inducing graphics was a series of paintings by Maira Kalman depicting a variety of "typical New Yorkers" as well as several of the actual behind-the-scenes personnel who make Grand Central function.

The popularity of the murals made their adaptation in picture-book form a natural. "I was so in love with the process of standing in this very romantic, epic structure," Kalman recalls, "watching people go about their business, that I felt I had to put it all in a book."

By now you will have noticed the Main Concourse's cerulean blue ceiling (painted by Paul Helleu; 1912). After the Hayden Planetarium [see page 81], this vast, 125-foot-high rendering of the night sky ranks as Manhattan's best view of the heavens, even if—incredible though it seems—the entire scene was mistakenly painted in reverse. How New York to attempt to fit the cosmos indoors! An entertaining young people's introduction to stargazing here or elsewhere is *Find the Constellations* (1954), by *Curious George* creator and one-time New Yorker, H.A. REY.

Grand Central contains numerous shops and eateries; the South Hall just off the Main Concourse plays host to changing art exhibitions. (For information about free tours: 212-935-3960; www.grandcentralterminal.com.)

When you are ready to leave the terminal, ascend the marble staircase at the western end of the Main Concourse and step out onto Vanderbilt Avenue. Look back at the station to notice the **Metropolitan Life Insurance Company** office tower perched incongruously atop the 1903–1913 Beaux-Arts terminal structure.

The former Pan Am Building, atop Grand Central Terminal

Known originally as the Pan Am Building (for the airline it headquartered when the tower first opened in 1963), this office building figures prominently in DIANE DUANE's ingeniously plotted fantasy adventure, *So You Want to Be a Wizard* (1983). It's from the Pan Am Building's rooftop (in fact once a futuristic heliport) that the story's two young protagonists, Nita Callahan and Kit Rodriguez, pass through an invisible "world gate" into a surreally terrifying alternate Manhattan.

As you cross Vanderbilt and follow East 43rd Street to Fifth Avenue, imagine yourself in that unremittingly dangerous other New York:

> *What had seemed a perfectly ordinary fire hydrant, dull yellow, with rust stains and peeling paint, suddenly cracked open and shot out a long, pale, ropy tongue like a toad's. The pigeon never had a chance. Hit side on, the bird made just one strangled gobbling noise before the tongue was gone again, too fast to follow, and the wide horizontal mouth it came from was closed again. All that remained to show that anything had happened was a slight bulge under the metallic-looking skin of the fire hydrant. The bulge heaved once and was still.* —So You Want to Be a Wizard

Cross Fifth Avenue and turn left, continuing south across 42nd Street. The impressive marble structure you see before you is **The New York Public Library** (212-661-7220; www.nypl.org).

The vital hub of a library system that encompasses eighty-five neighborhood branches in Manhattan, the Bronx, and Staten Island, the fabled "42nd Street Library" opened its doors to the public on May 24, 1911. Library service to children—still a novel concept at the turn of the century—was considered an important part of this library's mission from the start. The Central Children's Room—originally housed on the ground-floor level just to the left of the 42nd Street entrance—became a model of its kind for the nation and the world.

Although the Central Children's Room has long since migrated eleven blocks north to its present second-floor location in the Donnell Library Center at 20 West 53rd Street [see pages 53–54], it is well worth taking a moment to recall the original room and the history that was made there.

At a time when most American libraries admitted no one under the age of fourteen, New York's pioneering first superintendent of work with children, Anne Carroll Moore, asked only that a child seeking entry be able to sign his or her own name and present a clean pair of hands. Moore took great care in book selection, issued annual lists of the year's best offerings, and became a nationally respected critic and adviser to artists, writers, and editors in the field. Under her guidance, the children's collection, and staff, reflected the international makeup of New York's immigrant population. St. Nicholas Eve and the birthdays of Hans Christian Andersen and William Shakespeare were celebrated in the room, where exhibitions were held of original art by such luminaries of the illustrated book world as Walter Crane, Kate Greenaway, Arthur Rackham, and Wanda Gág.

Children entering by the 42nd Street entrance soon came to two adjoining rectangular rooms connected, as New York's second superintendent of work with children, Frances Clarke Sayers, recalled:

by an arched alcove stretching between. Here tables and chairs built for the picture-book set were in perfect proportion and the inset of a wide three-sided window seat, with polished wood paneling at the back and sides, offered a tempting area for sliding as well as an invitation to be seated. Here cherished old books of the past were housed in a glass-doored bookcase that stood against one wall.

Above it hung fine old English prints, the "Cries of London," and the portrait of an eighteenth-century duchess. . . . In the shelter of this many-cornered place, the smallest clientele found within hand's reach a choice of picture books for home borrowing.

The wider of the two rooms was given over to books for use in the library. . . . The Fifth Avenue window was set in an alcove that stood one step above the floor level. In the course of time, this became a proscenium, framing a succession of celebrations and celebrities: musicians, puppeteers, and poets; artists, editors, publishers; actors, playwrights, and magicians; storytellers and ballad singers . . .

On May 24, 1911, Mary Alice Murray became the first child to read aloud the following pledge and to sign her name in the New York Public Library Central Children's Room's registration book: *"When I write my name in this book I promise to take good care of the books I use in the Library and at home, and to obey the rules of the Library."*

One of the finest storytellers to cast her spell at the Central Children's Room was RUTH SAWYER, winner of the 1937 Newbery Medal for **Roller Skates**, her autobiographical novel of turn-of-the-century New York life, illustrated by VALENTI ANGELO (1936).

Set in 1890s Manhattan, *Roller Skates* recalls an eventful year in the life of brave, inquisitive 10-year-old Lucinda Wyman, whose parents have left her in the

Roller Skates, *by Ruth Sawyer, illustrated by Valenti Angelo*

care of family friends. Exploring the city on her own with an enviable lack of concern for her personal safety, Lucinda mingles with a broad cross section of the city's residents, from garrulous Patrolman M'Gonegal and the struggling Browdowski family of eastern European émigrés to famed New York confectioner Louis Sherry and her own aristocratic Uncle Earle.

The stretch of West 42nd Street starting at Fifth Avenue and running the length of Bryant Park is the heart of Patrolman M'Gonegal's beat. It is at the Fifth Avenue end of this block that a skating Lucinda first catches the officer's attention, "as a child of society, going down the avenue," on her way to and from the exclusive Miss Brackett's private school.

He had been waiting for a week to pick Lucinda's acquaintance when she gave him the chance by catching her skate on the curb and plunging headlong into the traffic of the street.

She let out a yelp like a frightened puppy and Patrolman M'Gonegal held up two delivery carts, pulled her to her feet, set her down upon the opposite curb, and asked: "Hurt?"

"Not a mite. The breath's just blown out of me." She looked down at the pongee pinafore. "That's ruined. Glory be to God, I can go one day without it." —Roller Skates

Foremost among Lucinda's new friends is Tony Coppino, an Italian immigrant boy who tends his father's produce stand a few blocks to the northwest of Bryant Park, at Eighth Avenue and West 46th Street. By 1930, Italian Americans represented 17 percent of the city's population and were doing a bit better economically than had those of the previous generation. In the more rigidly ethnocentric and class-conscious New York of the 1890s, Lucinda's open-minded regard for the honest, hardworking Tony and his family would have set her apart from many of her peers. In marked contrast, by the time Ruth Sawyer wrote *Roller Skates*, New York was governed by a popular mayor, Fiorello H. La Guardia, who was himself of Italian immigrant descent.

Now walk one block south to inspect the library's

magnificent Fifth Avenue facade, where the grand marble stairway, visibly worn by the footfalls of millions of patrons, is flanked by sculptor Edward Potter's festive library lions.

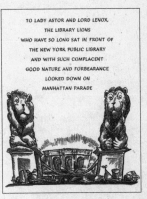

TO LADY ASTOR AND LORD LENOX,
THE LIBRARY LIONS
WHO HAVE SO LONG SAT IN FRONT OF
THE NEW YORK PUBLIC LIBRARY
AND WITH SUCH COMPLACENT
GOOD NATURE AND FORBEARANCE
LOOKED DOWN ON
MANHATTAN PARADE

Andy and the Lion,
by James Daugherty

These kingly cats, which serve as the central building's unofficial honor guard, inspired artist JAMES DAUGHERTY's first picture book, a free-form adaptation of the Greek legend of Androcles and the lion. *Andy and the Lion: A Tale of Kindness Remembered, or the Power of Gratitude* (1938), follows the adventures of an all-American lad who, after borrowing a book about lions from his local library, meets and befriends a real lion the very next day.

Daugherty set his gentle tale of kindness rewarded in a typical American small town, but he paid tribute to the New York Public Library's lions on the dedication page, addressing them as "Lord Lenox and Lady Astor," names that recall James Lenox and the family of John Jacob Astor, benefactors instrumental in the New York Public Library's founding in 1895. The artist was having his fun—both bushy-maned big cats are obviously male. The lions are also affectionately known as Patience (left) and Fortitude, names given them by Mayor La Guardia as inspiration for Depression-era New Yorkers.

The 42nd Street Library was built on a site once used by the city as a potter's field and later walled in and flooded to create the Croton Reservoir. In 1853, on the land just behind the library and now occupied by Bryant Park, New York's Crystal Palace opened in an impressive display of the industrial age's greatest achievements in the sciences and arts. In 1858 this imposing glass- and cast-iron exhibition hall burned to the ground.

Free tours of the New York Public Library are given Mon.–Sat. at 11 A.M. and 2 P.M. For information, call: 212-930-0830.

Take a few moments to explore **Bryant Park**, named for William Cullen Bryant (1794–1878), poet, newspaper editor, and advocate on behalf of such important civic institutions as Central Park and the Metropolitan Museum of Art. When this elegant green space, which serves as midtown Manhattan's front lawn, was redesigned in 1992, one of the artworks added was Jo Davidson's Buddha-like bronze portrait of *Gertrude Stein*, which can be found in the park's southeastern quadrant, near the entrance to the Bryant Park Grill. Although Stein herself never lived in New York, she became a major inspiration for a writer who did—MARGARET WISE BROWN. In 1939, Brown, then employed as the editor of the small New York house of William R. Scott and Company, published Stein's only children's book, *The World Is Round*, with illustrations by future *Goodnight Moon* artist CLEMENT HURD.

Gertrude Stein,
by Jo Davidson

Bryant Park is an important place in the life of Chester Cricket, the hero of GEORGE SELDEN's *The Cricket in Times Square* (1960), illustrated by GARTH WILLIAMS, and of a series of subsequent books including *Chester Cricket's Pigeon Ride* (1981).

Chester is a Connecticut country cricket who comes to New York trapped inside a picnic basket. Despite many and varied adventures in the big city, he misses the fresh air and freedom of the great outdoors. Then one evening, in *Chester Cricket's Pigeon Ride*, he emerges from a subway tunnel in Times Square, to the west of Bryant Park, and catches the blissful, fragrant scent of . . . a tree!

He sniffed again. And a sycamore at that—one of his favorites. He hadn't been near a tree for so long he'd forgotten what one smelled like! —*Chester Cricket's Pigeon Ride*

Making desperate hopping motions as he dodges evening traffic, Chester follows his cricket nose east from Times Square along 42nd Street, until he comes to the small but utterly welcoming rectangle of greenery where you are now standing:

His last jump landed him—plop!—on real earth. It felt so good to dig his feet down into it. For two weeks now, he'd been jumping on concrete, on asphalt, and steel, but never on dirt. And it had made his legs quite sore. But now he was resting on the lovely springy soil itself.

Chester Cricket's Pigeon Ride,
*by George Selden,
illustrated by
Garth Williams*

Poet William Cullen Bryant, who once wrote, "Go forth, under the open sky, and list to Nature's teachings . . ." would have understood Chester's feelings perfectly.

What really makes Bryant Park special for Chester, however, is that it is here he meets a pigeon named Lulu, who offers to take him on a whirlwind tour of Manhattan. Their first stop—and our next one—is the **Empire State Building.** To get there, walk back to Fifth Avenue and continue south to 34th Street. Enter between 33rd and 34th Streets and follow the signs for access to the Observation Tower. The Tower ticket office is open daily from 9:30 A.M. to 11:30 P.M. (For information, call 877-NYC-VIEW or visit www.esbnyc.com.)

Why do skyscrapers so excite our imagination? As we leave Chester and Lulu to their aerial adventures, consider what their creator, George Selden, had to say about this:

Now, it is strange, but it is true, that although there are many mountains higher than even the tallest buildings, and airplanes can fly much higher than mountains, nothing ever seems quite so high as a big building that's been built by men. It suggests our own height to ourselves, I guess.

The Empire State Building—for over forty years the world's tallest building—is one of New York's best-loved sights and symbols. Constructed in record time between 1930 and 1931 as the Great Depression deepened all around, its sleek, rocketlike "mooring mast," perched atop the tower's eighty-sixth story, was intended for use by dirigibles. (Only two dirigibles ever tried to tie up there; today, more people remember King Kong's wild embrace of the tower's silvery crown, in the 1933 film.) A 200-foot television antenna was added in 1953.

Countless children's book authors and illustrators have found a place for the Empire State Building in their stories. In *Sid & Sol* (1977), written by ARTHUR YORINKS, an oafish giant named Sol roams the land, causing the earth to tremble every time he laughs. To show just what a giant Sol is, illustrator RICHARD EGIELSKI depicts him standing head and shoulders over "the world's tallest building"—the Empire State Building.

James and the Giant Peach,
by Roald Dahl,
re-illustrated by Quentin Blake

And in ROALD DAHL's *James and the Giant Peach* (1961), re-illustrated by QUENTIN BLAKE (1995), a huge peach with a lonely boy and some newfound friends riding inside, rolls out of an English garden and off on a series of far-flung adventures. In the climactic scene, the peach and its passengers fly to New York City, borne improbably aloft by a flock of seagulls. After being mistaken for an incoming enemy bomb—Dahl was writing at the height of the cold war, a year before the Cuban missile crisis—the peach lands smack on the Empire State Building's television needle. James and friends emerge from within to a hero's welcome.

A wordless picture book with fiendishly adept and

dreamlike art, *Sector 7* by DAVID WIESNER (1999) begins as the story of a typical class trip to the Empire State Building's eighty-sixth-story observation deck. Then, something unexpected happens up there in the clouds. One child, singled out for his talent as an artist, is secretly whisked away and transported, as if by magic, to a factory in the sky—Sector 7—where clouds

Sector 7, *by David Wiesner*

are made, and where the boy is given the chance to try his hand at designing some. Wiesner cleverly arranges things so that the boy, after having the inspirational thrill of his life, rejoins his group with no one the wiser about his adventure. Wiesner based his depiction of the Cloud Dispatch Center on three New York landmarks: the old Pennsylvania Station and the Third Avenue Car Barns (both no longer standing), and Grand Central Terminal.

Three books shine a light on the famous skyscraper's construction. In *Unbuilding* (1980), DAVID MACAULAY does so ironically, by describing the work that would be entailed in the building's total dismantling—for reassembly in some unnamed, oil-rich desert nation. In 1980, Macaulay's fantasy did not seem entirely far-fetched, as many Americans were just becoming aware of the increasingly interdependent nature of the global economy. Beyond the book's satirical intent, *Unbuilding* offers a detailed look at the iconic structure's inner workings.

LEWIS W. HINE's *Men at Work* (1932), which photographically records the Empire State Building's construction, has long been considered one of American photography's classic documentary essays. What is often forgotten about this exhilarating photo-essay about workingmen in high and scary places, however, is that it was originally published as a children's book—as a collection of photos meant to share with modern children the story of one of the modern world's wonders. A picture book that incorporates Hine's photographs and other contemporary visuals in a narrative tracing one young construction worker's role in the epic undertaking is *Joe and the Skyscraper*, by DIETRICH NEUMANN (1999).

Exit the Empire State Building at West 34th Street and walk one long block west to **Herald Square**, an important crossroads named for a newspaper whose offices were once located here.

> *"This place is definitely not like my hometown," Frank tells us. "When I was really little the only things that I knew about New York came from the old songs that my parents listened to, like* New York, New York *and* Give My Regards to Broadway. . . . *I never got that song right. I thought that the words were* Remember me to Harold Square, *like Harold was some big-shot like the mayor or something."*
>
> *I giggle. "It's* Herald *Square—what they call the area near Macy's."* —Remember Me to Harold Square

In PAULA DANZIGER's valentine to New York, *Remember Me to Harold Square* (1987), a teenager visiting from the Midwest spends a memorable summer exploring Manhattan with two young native New Yorkers, who find that they too have much to learn about their city.

In *Milly and the Macy's Parade*, illustrated by BRETT HELQUIST (2002), SHANA COREY offers a largely fictionalized account of the original inspiration for the Macy's Thanksgiving Day Parade, a New York tradition since 1924. It is here, at Macy's, that Kris Kringle performs his holiday magic in VALENTINE DAVIES's *Miracle on 34th Street* (1947). This is also where the venturesome boy featured in AMOS VOGEL's *How Little Lori Visited Times Square*, illustrated by MAURICE SENDAK (1963), gets sidetracked during his preposterously roundabout journey uptown—and is helped on his way by a courteous New York turtle!

Like Lori, you may well wish to continue on to **Times Square.** The simplest way is to walk north along Broadway to 42nd Street. The dramatically tidied-up "crossroads of the world" has little in common visually, apart from the general bigness of things and the crowds, with the hurly-burly setting of George Selden's *The Cricket in Times Square*. Nonetheless, as you begin your exploration of this entertainment and tourist destination, take a moment to listen. Like Tucker Mouse, you might be surprised by what you hear:

Now Tucker Mouse had heard almost all the sounds that can be heard in New York City. He had heard the rumble of subway trains and the shriek their iron wheels make when they go around a corner. From above, through the iron grills that open onto the streets, he had heard the thrumming of the rubber tires of automobiles, and the hooting of their horns, and the howling of their brakes. And he had heard the babble of voices when the station was full of human beings, and the barking of dogs that some of them had on leashes. Pigeons, the birds of New York, and cats, and even the high purring of airplanes above the city Tucker had heard. But in all his days, and on all his journeys through the greatest city in the world, Tucker had never heard a sound quite like this one.
—*The Cricket in Times Square*

What was it that Tucker heard? Why, the Cricket in Times Square, of course.

The Cricket in Times Square,
by George Selden,
illustrated by Garth Williams

WALKING TOUR II

Start at the New York Public Library lions [see page 45] and, crossing 42nd Street, walk north along Fifth Avenue, the towering, store-lined thoroughfare that novelist Irwin Shaw once called New York's "street of dreams."

As you make your way up Fifth Avenue between 48th

and 49th Streets, take a moment to notice the building on the east side of the street at number 597, which for many years served as the headquarters and shop of the **Charles Scribner's Sons** publishing company. Founded in New York in 1846, Scribner moved uptown to this building in 1913. It was from here that all but the first of **N.C. Wyeth**'s Scribner Illustrated Classics emanated. Scribner published such later notable children's books as **Marjorie Kinnan Rawlings**'s *The Yearling* (1938) and the work of three-time Caldecott Medal–winner **Marcia Brown**. If you look closely above the great third-floor arched window, you will see the original bronze Scribner plaque flanked by cherubs. Marcia Brown incorporated these cherubs in the illustration that appears opposite the title page of her first Caldecott winner, *Cinderella* (1954).

Now on the west side of Fifth Avenue, between 49th and 50th Streets, take time to wander into the Rockefeller Center **Promenade** (officially called the **Channel Gardens**). Set among the exquisite seasonal plantings of this elegant pedestrian passageway are six bronze fountainhead sculptures of mythic *Triton* and *Nereids* riding the backs of dolphins. Dating from 1935, they are the work of René Paul Chambellan, the sculptor who designed both the Newbery and Caldecott Medals. On your right as you head into the Promenade is the British

Triton, *by René Paul Chambellan*

Empire Building, on the exterior wall of which is a striking bas-relief depiction of the Greek messenger god *Hermes* (also the god of commerce, travel, and thievery!).

The Rockefeller family, who had made their fortune in oil and banking a generation earlier, built this resplendent Art Deco–style office, shopping, and entertainment complex between 1932 and 1940. Public artworks placed throughout the center feature mythological subjects, suggesting a flattering comparison to modern man's— or was it just the Rockefellers'?—storied achievements. One of the city's most popular outdoor sculptures,

Paul Manship's golden *Prometheus* (1934) astride Mount Olympus, can be viewed from the end of the Promenade. From his high perch, Prometheus presides over the center's winter skating rink/ warm-weather outdoor restaurant.

Prometheus,
by Paul Manship

Returning to Fifth Avenue, walk north, stopping at the entrance to 630 Fifth Avenue to view another Rockefeller Center icon, Lee Lawrie's 15-foot-high bronze *Atlas* (1937). In Greek mythology, Atlas is the titan condemned by Zeus to bear the weight of the heavens on his shoulders. For readers interested in knowing more about this story and the others that inspired the center's monumental art, Ingri and Edgar Parin d'Aulaire's *D'Aulaires' Book of Greek Myths* (1962) remains unsurpassed as a young people's introduction.

Continuing north along Fifth Avenue, turn left onto 53rd Street and continue for half a block to the **Donnell Library Center** of the New York Public Library (20 West 53rd Street; 212-621-0636; www.nypl.org). Take the elevator to the second-floor **Central Children's Room.** Here, in addition to one of the city's finest collections of contemporary and historical children's books, you will find a permanent display of the room's treasures as well as changing exhibitions of books and related art and artifacts. Among the rare items always on view are original paintings by N.C. Wyeth; P.L. Travers's own Mary Poppins parrot-handle umbrella; and, perhaps most notable of all, the original toy bear and other stuffed animals belonging to Christopher Milne—the inspiration for A.A. Milne's Pooh books. Visitors from around the world come each day for a look at the patched but imperishable Pooh, Eeyore, Tigger, and their friends. Take a moment to browse through and sign the Pooh guest book. One floor below, on the mezzanine level, is the

Nathan Straus Room, the city's largest collection of young-adult books and related library materials of interest to teens (212-621-0633).

Directly across from the library is the **Museum of Modern Art** (11 West 53rd Street; 212-708-9400; www.moma.org), which, in keeping with its core commitment to explore the interrelationship between the "applied" and "fine" arts, occasionally includes illustrated children's books in its exhibitions. (Please note that while major renovation work continues through early 2005, the museum has relocated to temporary quarters in Long Island City, Queens; for hours and directions, call the telephone number above or consult the museum's website.)

The museum, affectionately known by its acronym as MOMA, is the setting of the culminating scene of Neil Waldman's picture-book fantasy, *The Starry Night* (1999). Named for a painting by Vincent van Gogh in

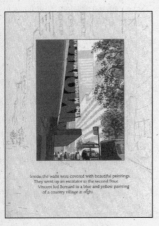

The Starry Night,
by Neil Waldman

MOMA's collection, the story imagines a time-travel visit by Vincent himself to modern-day Manhattan. Moving anonymously through the city, van Gogh befriends a boy named Bernard, who stands fascinated while the artist paints beside the toy boat pond in Central Park [see pages 58–60] and at various other Manhattan locales. At van Gogh's suggestion, MOMA is their final stop. On seeing the painting *The Starry Night*, Bernard, without having to be told, immediately recognizes it as the work of his mysterious acquaintance.

Return to Fifth Avenue, cross to the east side, and continuing two blocks north, turn right at 55th Street, stopping at the **St. Regis Hotel** (2 East 55th Street). On entering, climb the few steps to the lobby level and bear left past the Astor Court restaurant until you reach the

King Cole Lounge. Because the Lounge is a bar, it is best to time your visit for the late morning or early afternoon, before the day's serious drinking begins. The reason for your visit will be immediately apparent: artist Maxfield Parrish's dazzlingly painted 1906 mural, which spans the far wall with larger-than-life images of the original "merry old soul" of Mother Goose fame and his courtiers.

Return to Fifth Avenue, crossing back to the west side, and walk north until you come to the formal open space called Grand Army Plaza and—just to the left—**The Plaza Hotel** (768 Fifth Avenue), home of KAY THOMPSON and HILARY KNIGHT's *Eloise* (1955).

Entering The Plaza by the revolving door immortalized in Knight's red-pink-black-and-white drawings, you will find yourself in the familiar-looking lobby and recognize just ahead the **Palm Court** where, like Eloise, you may decide to have lunch or possibly afternoon tea. The mail desk, ballrooms, and elevators are all pretty much as Hilary Knight drew them. The ground-floor *Eloise* gift shop is a more recent addition. By following the lobby corridor

Eloise, *by Kay Thompson, illustrated by Hilary Knight*

to the left and turning right at the end of the passageway, you will soon come to that shop, and to the **oil portrait of Eloise** that Knight presented as a birthday gift to his collaborator on November 9, 1964. Thompson in turn gave the painting to the hotel, where she herself was a resident when she dreamed up her timeless 6-year-old.

CENTRAL PARK ■ UPPER EAST SIDE

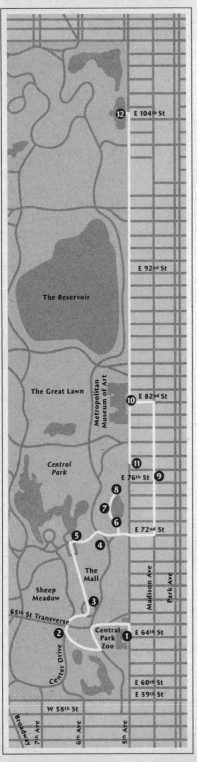

▼ Walking Tour II

1. 436 & 438 E. 88th St. (Lyle the Crocodile's neighborho●
2. E. 87th St. & East End Ave. (Harriet Welsch townhouse)
3. Carl Schurz Park / Peter Pan
4. Chapin School (100 East End Ave●
5. 524 E. 85th St. (Louise Fitzhugh a●
6. 444 E. 82nd St. (Ezra Jack Keats a●
7. Webster Branch of NYPL

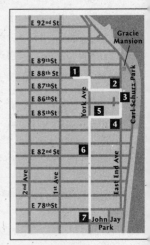

◀ Walking Tour I

1. Central Park Zoo
2. Friedsom Memorial Carousel
3. Literary Walk / Mall
4. Mother Goose statue
5. Bethesda Fountain
6. Conservatory Water
7. *Hans Christian Andersen* statue
8. *Alice in Wonderland* statue
9. Hotel Carlyle / Bemelmans Bar
10. The Metropolitan Museum of A●
11. 972 5th Ave. (*Marble Boy* statue)
12. Conservatory Garden / Francis Hodgson Burnett Founta●

CENTRAL PARK

■

UPPER EAST SIDE

WALKING TOUR I

*E*nter Central Park at Fifth Avenue and 59th Street (Fifth Avenue station of the N line) and follow the walkway north. You will soon come to the **Central Park Zoo**, at 64th Street. Plan to arrive just before the top of the hour, when the chimes of the *Delacorte Clock* (Andrea Spadini, sculptor; 1965) ring out such familiar nursery-rhyme songs as "Hickory, Dickory, Dock" and "Three Blind Mice." In

Delacorte Clock, *by Andrea Spadini*

YUMI HEO's *One Sunday Morning* (1999), a small boy and his father take the subway to the park and spend the better part of a glorious morning having a good look at this zoo's sea lions, polar bears, monkeys, and indoor penguin and tropical rain-forest exhibitions.

Return to the southern end of the zoo, exit, and, turning right, follow the broad East Drive north a short distance to the Wollman Rink. Take the footpath west past the rink to Center Drive, and follow it north until you come to the **Friedsam Memorial Carousel** (open

One Sunday Morning, *by Yumi Heo*

10:30 A.M.–6 P.M. daily; closes at 5 P.M. during the winter), with its fifty-seven carved wooden horses. KATHY JAKOB-

SEN captures this festive scene in one of the many intricately detailed, faux-primitive paintings of *My New York* (1993).

From the carousel, take the footpath leading north and watch, in the near distance to your right, for the beginning of the **Literary Walk**, a northward footpath featuring sculptures of William Shakespeare, Sir Walter Scott, and others. Follow the Literary Walk as it flows into the **Mall**, and continuing almost to the end, take the path off to the right leading to the **Mary Harriman Rumsey Playfield**. Walk to

My New York,
by Kathy Jakobsen

the far end to find Central Park's granite sculpture of *Mother Goose* (F.G.R. Roth, sculptor; 1938). When you are ready to continue, retrace your steps to the Mall and continue onward straight ahead across 72nd Street Drive to the magnificent **Bethesda Fountain**, where, in RICHARD EGIELSKI's uproarious retelling of *The Gingerbread Boy* (1997), the spry confectionery lad at last runs out of luck and is eaten by a fox.

Returning to 72nd Street Drive, walk east, watching for the footpath that trails off to the left and down Pilgrim Hill to the **Conservatory Water**, the neo-Renaissance concrete basin immortalized in E.B. WHITE's *Stuart Little* (1945).

E.B. White made his mark during the 1920s as one of *The New*

Mother Goose,
by F.G.R. Roth

The Gingerbread Boy,
by Richard Egielski

Yorker magazine's finest and funniest essayist/reporters. His wife, Katharine, edited fiction and reviewed children's books at *The New Yorker* for many years, but it was at the suggestion of the New York Public Library's Anne Carroll Moore that White attempted to write his first fantasy for children.

It took White more than seven years to complete *Stuart Little*, his quirky tale about a mouse-child born into an ordinary family of Manhattanites. By the time he did so, the 6-year-old niece he had hoped to amuse with it had grown into a teenager—and was reading Hemingway! Ironically, Anne Carroll Moore (by then retired but still a powerful critic) disliked White's story so intensely

Conservatory Water, Central Park

that she urged him not to publish it. He went ahead anyway, of course, also helping to choose the perfect illustrator—GARTH WILLIAMS—a London-trained newcomer whose entertaining work for *The New Yorker* had caught the author's attention.

*When the bus stopped at Seventy-second Street, Stuart
jumped out and hurried across to the sailboat pond in Central Park. . . .*

*When the people . . . learned that one of the toy sailboats
was being steered by a mouse in a sailor suit, they all came
running. . . .*

*"This is the life for me!" Stuart murmured to himself.
"What a ship! What a day! What a race!"*

—Stuart Little

Just west of the toy boat pond stands the **Hans Christian
Andersen** statue, (George J. Lober, sculptor; Otto F.

Langmann, architect; 1956). Every Saturday at 11 A.M. from May through
September, a free program of children's
stories by Andersen and others is per-
formed here. (For information: 212-
360-2752.) A biography of this writer
for children that reveals his far less
well-known talent as a visual artist is
BETH WAGNER BRUST's *The Amazing
Paper Cuttings of Hans Christian Andersen* (1994).

Hans Christian Andersen,
by George J. Lober

Directly north and also within sight
of the boat pond is the *Alice in Wonderland Margarita Delacorte Memorial* playground sculpture (José de Creeft, sculptor; 1959), based on the classic
SIR JOHN TENNIEL illustrations for LEWIS CARROLL's most
famous book. Here, cast in bronze and scaled for climbing,
are the ever curious Alice herself flanked by the Mad
Hatter, the March Hare,
the Dormouse, and the
Cheshire Cat. *The Other
Alice*, by CHRISTINA
BJORK and INGA-KARIN
ERIKSSON (1993), pres-
ents a many-faceted por-
trait of Carroll and Alice
Liddell, the young dau-
ghter of an Oxford dean

Alice in Wonderland Margarita Delacor
Memorial, *by José de Creeft*

Curiouser and Curiouser: Alice in New York

Although the Rev. Charles Dodgson—who wrote for children under the pen name Lewis Carroll—never visited the United States, New York is nonetheless one of the best places to learn more about the Oxford don and his literary creations. The IRT local subway station at Broadway and West 50th Street features a series of original ceramic mosaics titled **"Alice: The Way Out,"** by artist Liliana Porter (1994). Depicted along the walls are the Queen of Hearts, Mad Hatter, Alice, and—in true New York fashion "late for a very important date"—the White Rabbit.

Alice: The Way Out,
by Liliana Porter

The Lewis Carroll Room, Fales Library, New York University (70 Washington Square South, open by appointment; 212-998-2599), houses a charming display of rare Carrolliana, including letters, manuscripts, *Alice* editions, photographs taken by the author, and much more. Both the **New York Public Library** (Fifth Avenue and 42nd Street; 212-930-0801) and the **Pierpont Morgan Library** (29 East 36th Street at Madison Avenue; 212-685-0610) own original art and manuscripts relating to Carroll that are occasionally put on public view.

at whose prompting Carroll created his immortal tale.

Leave the park at the East 72nd Street exit, officially known as Inventor's Gate. Walk east, past Fifth Avenue to Madison and proceed north to the **Hotel Carlyle** (35 East 76th Street). Enter and follow the signs to the **Bemelmans Bar**, with its fanciful murals of Central Park by the creator of *Madeline*.

Austrian-born LUDWIG BEMELMANS was a self-taught artist who came to New York at age sixteen. Working for a time as a hotel busboy, he eventually became the owner of Hapsburg House, a midtown restaurant popular with publishers. Among the regulars was May Massee, children's book editor of the Viking Press. When at a private party at Bemelmans's apartment, Massee noticed the amusing paintings with which he had covered his window shades for the sake of the "view," she urged her host and friend to redirect his talents to book illustration. In the years that followed, Bemelmans became famous not only as a picture-book author and illustrator but also as a *New Yorker* cover artist and travel writer.

Known equally for his creative flair and personal extravagance, Bemelmans often found himself short of money. He painted the Carlyle murals—in which mischievous Madeline, her classmates, and the stern but tolerant Miss Clavel can also be seen to the left of the bar—in 1947, in exchange for a year and a half's free lodging for himself and his family. It is best to stop in at off-hours; for information, call 212-744-1600.

Continue up Madison Avenue to 82nd Street, then, crossing to the west side of the street, walk one more block west until you come to **The Metropolitan Museum of Art** (Fifth Avenue and 82nd Street; Tues.–Thurs. & Sun.: 9:30 A.M.–5:30 P.M.; Fri. & Sat. 9:30 A.M.–9:00 P.M.; 212-879-5500; www.metmuseum.org).

If you think of doing something in New York City,
you can be certain that at least two thousand other people
have that same thought. And of the two thousand who do,
about one thousand will be standing in line waiting to do it.
—From the Mixed-up Files of Mrs. Basil E. Frankweiler

E.L. KONIGSBURG's irreverent Newbery Medal–winning novel *From the Mixed-up Files of Mrs. Basil E. Frankweiler* (1967) tells the story of a boldly enterprising suburban brother and sister, Claudia (age 12) and Jamie (age 9), who run away from home and hide out for a week in the Metropolitan Museum.

Finding a good place to sleep undetected is among their first challenges.

They wandered back to the rooms of fine French and English furniture. It was Claudia who knew for sure that she had chosen the most elegant place in the world to hide. She wanted to sit on the lounge chair that had been made for Marie Antoinette or at least sit at her writing table. But signs everywhere said not to step on the platform.
— *From the Mixed-up Files of Mrs. Basil E. Frankweiler*

Extravagant Queen Marie Antoinette was the wife of Louis XVI of France. Like her husband, she was among those beheaded during the early days of the French Revolution.

From the Mixed-up Files of Mrs. Basil E. Frankweiler, *by E.L. Konigsburg*

To see the royal writing table that so impressed Claudia, enter the museum galleries via the Great Hall's central admission counter and bear left until you come to the Wrightsman Galleries of European decorative arts. Proceed to the **Formal Reception Room from the Hôtel de Tessé**, Paris. The marble, bronze, and lacquered oak "secretary," as such tables are known, can be found in the far right-hand corner of this period room. (The queen's matching commode is across the room to the left!)

Exit the Wrightsman Galleries, returning to the central corridor, which doubles as the main pathway through the museum's **Medieval Galleries**. Pay a brief visit to the **Chapel** (straight ahead just past the archway, as you walk back toward the Great Hall) where Claudia and Jamie kneel to say the Lord's Prayer—and ask forgiveness for having pinched a much-needed copy of *The New York Times*.

As you leave the Chapel alcove, take the first right and continue on until you reach the entrance to the museum's fabled **Department of Arms and Armor**, the full-dress display of medieval weaponry and warrior apparel that appeals more to romantic Claudia than to pragmatic Jamie.

> *Claudia hid her violin case . . . in a beautifully carved Roman marble sarcophagus.*   —*From the Mixed-up Files . . .*

The word *sarcophagus* means "fiesh eater." The ancient Romans buried their dead in these often elaborately carved stone coffins. Claudia most likely chose as her storage locker a sarcophagus like the rather grand marble example, dating from circa A.D. 130–150, on display in the Roman antiquities gallery. Find this gallery by returning to the Great Hall. Reenter the museum by the south admission desk and walk straight ahead to the gallery just before and to the right of the entrance to the cafeteria.

Directly across from the corridor from the Roman

Reference photo of the Fountain at the Met, *by E.L. Konigsburg*

antiquities gallery is the **Men's Room** where Jamie hides each afternoon just before closing time, to elude the museum guards. (It's been changed into a Women's Room; the men's lavatory is now one flight up.) Just beyond lies the **Museum Cafeteria** in whose fountain (now drained of water and transformed into a second, more upscale eatery) Jamie and Claudia bathe and collect coins for pocket money.

> *Since we can't learn everything about the Italian Renaissance today, let's learn everything about the Egyptian room.*
>   —*From the Mixed-up Files . . .*

Returning to the Great Hall, you will see, directly across from the Greek and Roman galleries, the entrance to the museum's spectacular **Egyptian Wing**. Among the treasures that Claudia and Jamie make sure not to miss is the

Tomb of Perneb, circa 2450 B.C., which stands just beyond the entranceway to the Egyptian galleries. Once you have explored the tomb with its interior walls covered from floor to ceiling with hieroglyphs, follow the galleries off to the right until you come to Gallery 8, where the **jewelry of Princess Sithhathoryunet**, circa 1897–1797 B.C., are displayed—along with the rest of the Treasure of Lahun. Then continue through the galleries at your own pace, taking care to stop at Gallery 28 to inspect the **bronze sculpture of a cat**, dating from the Macedonian or Ptolemaic period circa 332–305 B.C. or 305–30 B.C.

The area of the museum where the children spend the most time, the **Italian Renaissance galleries**, can be reached by again returning to the Great Hall, choosing the central entranceway, and proceeding up the grand staircase. At the top of the stairs, enter the Sackler Gallery and walk straight ahead and to the right.

The object that most intrigues Claudia and Jamie during their weeklong adventure is a marble sculpture of a boy, called *Angel*, which, as the children learn, is believed by some experts to be the work of the great Italian Renaissance sculptor Michelangelo. The children devote much of their time to finding out, detective-style, whether or not this is so.

Visitors hoping to see Angel for themselves will be disappointed, as the museum has never owned such a sculpture. Konigsburg created it in her own imagination. But the story does not end there. By an amazing coincidence, unbeknownst to the author of *From the Mixed-up Files*, a quite similar sculpture of a cupid or boy, on display for decades in a building just a few blocks south of the museum, was tentatively identified in 1996 as a long-lost work of . . . Michelangelo! To see this newly recognized art treasure, turn right as you exit the museum and walk south to the cultural services office of the French Embassy, at **number 972** (between East 77th and 78th Streets; 212-439-1400). Enter the lobby, where the Renaissance *Marble Boy* awaits you.

Head north on Fifth Avenue to 104th Street. As you

More About the Met

You Can't Take a Balloon into the Metropolitan Museum, by JACQUELINE PREISS WEITZMAN; illustrated by ROBIN PREISS GLASSER (1998). In this witty and

You Can't Take a Balloon into the Metropolitan Museum,
by Jacqueline Preiss Weitzman,
illustrated by Robin Preiss Glasser

richly detailed wordless book, a young girl tours the Met while the balloon she had checked at the door drifts all around town.

Fun with Hieroglyphs, by CATHARINE ROEHRIG (1990). A hands-on introduction to reading the writing on the Egyptian Wing's walls, with 24 rubber stamps, an ink pad, and guide to writing like a pharoah scribe.

Inside the Museum: A Children's Guide to the Metropolitan Museum of Art, by JOY RICHARDSON (1993). A lively guide and activity book that offers a closer look at a variety of the museum's treasures.

do so, think of the following passage from FRANCES HODGSON BURNETT's *The Secret Garden* (1911):

She took a long breath and looked behind her up the long walk to see if anyone was coming . . . She held back the swinging curtain of ivy and pushed back the door, which opened slowly—slowly.

Then she slipped through it. . . .
"How still it is!" she whispered. "How still."
— *The Secret Garden*

New York's own Secret Garden is our next and final destination. It is found within the beautifully kept six-acre **Conservatory Garden in Central Park**, just off Fifth Avenue between 104th and 105th Streets. Burnett drew inspiration for her classic novel from memories of an "enchanted garden" recalled from her childhood years in Manchester, England. As a teenager, she and her impoverished family moved to Tennessee, where, to help out financially, she began writing stories for magazines. Burnett spent much of the rest of her busy life shuttling by steamship between New York and London to meet with her publishers and oversee productions of the stage versions of her hugely popular books, which also included *Little Lord Fauntleroy* (1886) and *A Little Princess* (1905). American admirers of the author paid for the fountain sculpture, which depicts Mary Lennox and her country friend Dickon, as a tribute to her literary legacy.

Frances Hodgson Burnett
Memorial Fountain,
by Bessie Potter Vonnob

Free, family-oriented storytelling events are held on weekends during the warmer months at this exquisitely peaceful hideaway spot. For information, call the Central Park Conservancy: 212-860-1370.

WALKING TOUR II
Yorkville

Still a rural village in the early 1800s, the portion of Manhattan Island extending from Third Avenue to the East River, between 96th and 72nd Streets, became a thriving German-American community before the end of the nineteenth century. During the 1920s, luxury apartment houses and private schools rose on some of the choicer lots on or near the river. Further adding to the mix, Gracie Mansion, originally the home of one of the area's wealthiest early landowners, became the mayor's official residence in 1942.

During the 1960s, this quiet, out-of-the-way corner of Manhattan was a favorite strolling place for a designer at *Life* magazine named Bernard Waber. With three small children at home, Waber had already discovered the pleasures of storytelling when he wrote these words inspired in part by his Yorkville wanderings:

> *This is the house. The house on East 88th Street. It is empty now, but it won't be for long. Strange sounds come from the house. Can you hear them? Listen: SWISH, SWASH, SPLASH, SWOOSH . . .*
>
> —*The House on East 88th Street*

Who—or what—could create such a racket? Why, a *very* large reptile: Waber's talented and supremely good-natured crocodile, Lyle.

The House on East 88th Street (1962) was **BERNARD WABER**'s second children's book and the first of six to feature the Primm family and their endearing croc. Although Waber invented the Primm brownstone at his drawing table, one astute New York Public librarian has aptly pointed to the town houses at **436** and **438 East 88th Street,** between First and York Avenues, as very close real-world approximations. Lyle would *have* to live close to Gracie Mansion, Waber himself has said, because "he likes waving to the mayor." (No subway line services this part of town. To reach Lyle's house, consider taking the M15 bus north on First Avenue to East 89th Street and walk one block

The House on East 88th Street,
by Bernard Waber

south or the M86 bus east on East 86th Street to First Avenue and walking two blocks north.)

Lyle shares this neighborhood with Harriet M. Welsch, the rambunctious heroine of *Harriet the Spy*, written and illustrated by LOUISE FITZHUGH (1964).

Fitzhugh's novel shocked some early critics with its frank depiction of a moody, rebellious preteen girl. At age 11, Harriet walks with a slouch, scowls at her parents, and spies on the neighbors, all the while keeping a secret notebook in which she records her private observations.

> *The Robinsons were a couple who lived in a duplex on Eighty-eighth Street. When they were alone they never said a word to each other. Harriet liked to watch them when they had company, because it made her laugh to see them show-ing off their house. Because the Robinsons had only one problem. They thought they were perfect.*
>
> *Luckily, their living room was on the ground floor . . .*
> —Harriet the Spy

But if some critics were unsure, at first, what to make of Harriet's uncompromising man-ner, youngsters were quick to identify with the funny, feisty rebel who wears her heart on her sweatshirt sleeve.

The well-to-do Welsches live in a three-story private town house at **East 87th Street and East End Avenue**, across the street from Gracie Mansion. Fitzhugh does not specify the address, but the most likely house is the one at 558 East 87th Street. The third-floor windows under the eaves on the East End Avenue side are those of Harriet's own bedroom—and private bath!—looking out on **Carl Schurz Park**. The "Gregory School," where Harriet is a sixth grader, is modeled on the exclusive **Chapin School**, three blocks to the south at 100 East End Av-

Harriet the Spy,
by Louise Fitzhugh

enue at 84th Street (although Chapin has never admitted boys). Harriet's "spy route," details of which Fitzhugh left purposely vague, consists of shops and residences within a few blocks to the south and west of home. The novel's climactic scene, in which Harriet's classmates have it out with her after discovering that her notebook is peppered with criticisms of them, takes place in the park.

Peter Pan in New York

In 1975, more than a decade after Louise Fitzhugh imagined Harriet and her friends there, **Carl Schurz Park** became home to CHARLES ANDREW HAFNER'S 1928 **sculpture of Peter Pan.** The statue of the boy who vowed to "never grow up" was moved to the park in that year from its original site in the lobby of Times Square's Paramount Theater. In August 1998 a group of teen vandals managed to dislodge the one-thousand-pound, four-foot-eleven-inch sculpture from its pedestal and toss it into the East River. "There was a dent in the railing," a Franciscan priest who witnessed the incident later told a reporter. Thanks to that priest's sharp detective work, police scuba divers were able to recover New York's tribute to one of children's literature's best-loved troublemakers. To view the statue, enter the park at East 87th Street and follow the footpath straight back and through the stone arch.

Louise Fitzhugh was born in 1928 into a politically prominent Memphis, Tennessee, family. When her parents divorced while she was still just a baby, she became the focus of a bitter custody battle that in later years left her with a deep sense of abandonment that later informed her writing. In 1949, after dropping out of Bard College six months before graduation, she headed for Greenwich Village to write and paint. By the time she wrote *Harriet*, Fitzhugh was living uptown, in the garden apartment of the five-story brick row house at **524 East 85th Street** (between York and East End Avenues), within blocks of Harriet's home address. The alley across the street and a few steps west of the author's apartment, running between the apartment building at 509 and the storefront at 501, resembles the one where Harriet hides when spying on the Dei Santis's grocery.

Now as then, in both fiction and fact, Harriet's neighborhood ranks among Manhattan's most coveted addresses. Even so, not everyone who makes a home there—including Harriet's best friend, a suitably oddball boy called Sport—has money. Sport's father is a struggling writer, and the apartment that he and his son share is cramped and inadequate. In part because the writer's life is the one Harriet envisions for herself, she turns to her notebook to mull over this seemingly unfair fact of New York life.

> *SPORT'S HOUSE SMELLS LIKE OLD LAUNDRY, AND IT'S NOISY AND KIND OF POOR-LOOKING. MY HOUSE DOESN'T SMELL AND IS QUIET LIKE MRS. PLUMBER'S. DOES THAT MEAN WE ARE RICH? WHAT MAKES PEOPLE RICH OR POOR?*
>
> —*Harriet the Spy*

After exploring Fitzhugh's stretch of East 85th Street, turn left onto York Avenue and, continuing onward for three blocks, turn right onto East 82nd Street, watching for the high-rise apartment house at **number 444**. EZRA JACK KEATS, the 1963 Caldecott Medal winner for *The Snowy Day*, lived here, with splendid views of the East River, for the last several years of his life.

As an Upper East Sider, Keats frequented the **Webster branch** of the New York Public Library (1465 York Avenue; 212-288-5049). To get there, return to York Avenue and walk four blocks to East 78th Street. Watch for the library on the west side of the street just south of the intersection.

Keats's fondness for this literary outpost is still in evidence in the children's room in the form of a whimsical sign he painted for the library, a Keats drawing also on permanent display in the room, and a plaque honoring the artist's memory.

CENTRAL PARK ▪ UPPER WEST SIDE

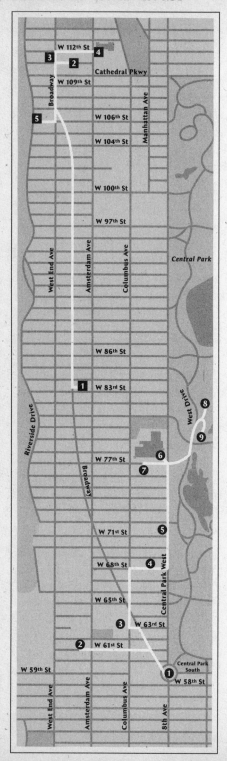

◀ **Walking Tour II**

1 Children's Museum of Manhattan

2 532 West 111th St. (Johanna Hurwitz apt.)

3 Bank Street College of Education

4 Cathedral of St. John the Divine

5 River Mansion

◀ **Walking Tour I**

1 Columbus Circle

2 Alvin Ailey American Dance Theater

3 Lincoln Center (Avery Fisher Hall / Metropolitan Opera Co. / Library for the Performing Arts / New York State Theater)

4 25 West 68th St. (Hatcher apartment)

5 115 Central Park West (Andrews apartment)

6 American Museum of Natural History / Hall of Ornithischian Dinosaurs / Rose Center for Earth and Space

7 16 West 77th St. / Astor Turret

8 Great Lawn

9 Belvedere Castle

CENTRAL PARK

■

UPPER WEST SIDE

So, we're going back, I thought. Back to the Big Apple. . . .
To some people there's no place like Nu Yuck. And I guess
I'm one of them. —Peter, in Superfudge, *by Judy Blume*

Our tour begins in **Columbus Circle**, by the Merchant's Gate entrance to **Central Park** (northeast corner of Central Park South and Central Park West). The A, B, C, D, 1, and 9 subway lines all stop here. This major Manhattan crossroads, where Broadway, Central Park West, Eighth Avenue, and 59th Street converge, acquired its name after a column and statue were erected here, in 1892 and 1894 respectively, to honor the explorer. Memorable picture-book views of the circle can be found in PETER SÍS's *Follow the Dream: The Story of Christopher Columbus* (1991) and *Under New York,* by LINDA OATMAN HIGH, illustrated by ROBERT RAYEVSKY (2001).

Under New York,
below skyscrapers and moonshine and sky,
there are stones and sand, clay, and lots of big rocks
made by glaciers,
millions of years ago.

Under New York, *by Linda Oatman High,*
illustrated by Robert Rayevsky

More Upper West Side Artists and Writers Over the Years

Russell Freedman • Mirra Ginsburg • M.B. Goffstein • Amy Hest • Deborah Hautzig • Esther Hautzig • June Jordon • Ellen Levine • Milton Meltzer • Margaret Miller • Roni Schotter • Janet Schulman • Isaac Bashevis Singer • Monica Wellington • Arthur Yorinks

Montague Mad-Rat the Younger, the hero of Tor Seidler's romantic adventure-fantasy *A Rat's Tale*, illustrated by Fred Marcellino (1986), passes through Columbus Circle often on his way to Central Park, where he scavenges for the berries and feathers that his hard-working milliner mother turns into "rat hats."

> *By the time Montague finally came out of the park onto Columbus Circle, his sleek gray fur was soaked, and he'd lost half his mother's feathers. Columbus Circle was in turmoil. Yellow cabs and delivery trucks were honking, and drenched people were rushing every which way, making it decidedly unpleasant to linger. But just as Montague was about to dive off the curb into the shelter of an underground drainpipe, something caught his sharp eyes. A prim pack of rats was stranded under the towering statue in the center of the Circle, huddled under brightly colored umbrellas. Montague was surprised: he'd never seen rats with umbrellas before.*
>
> —*A Rat's Tale*

Pause to look in at Central Park through the Merchant's Gate. As author Barbara Kerley and illustrator Brian Selznick reveal in *The Dinosaurs of Waterhouse Hawkins* (2001), in 1868 the parkland just to the north of this entrance was to have become the site of a museum unlike any that New Yorkers had yet seen or imagined.

In that year, English artist, naturalist, and showman Benjamin Waterhouse Hawkins came to New York to lecture on dinosaurs. It was Hawkins who had constructed

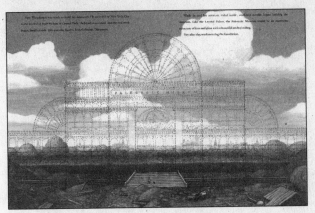

The Dinosaurs of Waterhouse Hawkins, *by Barbara Kerley,*
illustrated by Brian Selznick

the world's first life-sized models of the mammoth prehistoric creatures and exhibited them to great acclaim, in
1851, in London's Crystal Palace. So enthusiastic was the
American response to Hawkins's illustrated talks that
the head of Central Park proposed building a Paleozoic
Museum in the park's southwest corner as a home
for a permanent exhibition of the Englishman's models.
All seemed set when "Boss" William M. Tweed, the
powerful and notoriously corrupt politician who ruled
New York, abruptly scrapped plans for the Paleozoic.
Hawkins's clay-clad, iron-skeletoned creations were
scrapped, too. The dino parts were buried in Central Park
where, presumably, they still remain. Just where, exactly,
nobody knows!

> *They skated everywhere in the lower end of the Park,*
> *through the Merchant's Gate [Columbus Circle entrance],*
> *out the Artist's Gate [Central Park South at Sixth Avenue],*
> *in the Scholar's Gate [Fifth Avenue at 60th Street], and*
> *around the pond. They fed the goldfish; they coasted down*
> *the Mall. . . . They rode the musical horses in the carousel . . .*
> *They skated up to the Museum of Natural History and*
> *could never get their fill of it.* —*Roller Skates*

Now walk north along Broadway, pausing at West 61st
Street. Three blocks west, at 211 West 61st Street (between Amsterdam and West End Avenues), are the studio

The Philharmonic Gets Dressed, *by Karla Kuskin, illustrated by Marc Simont*

and offices of the **Alvin Ailey American Dance Theater**. ANDREA DAVIS PINKNEY introduces the life and exciting work of the company's founder in *Alvin Ailey* (1993), a picture book illustrated by BRIAN PINKNEY.

Return to Broadway and continue north to West 63rd Street, turn left and cross Columbus Avenue. You have now come to Manhattan's major performing-arts complex, **Lincoln Center**. *The Philharmonic Gets Dressed*, by KARLA KUSKIN, illustrated by MARC SIMONT (1982), surveys, in deadpan fashion, the pre-performance bathing, dressing, and travel routines of the members of a symphony orchestra very much like the New York Philharmonic. The Philharmonic's home, **Avery Fisher Hall**, is the spidery-columned neoclassical building to the right of the fountain as you face west.

Kuskin was married to an oboist at the time she wrote this wonderfully offbeat picture book and knew firsthand that children are just as curious about the formal finery (and underwear!) of concert musicians as they are about their music-making. In the book's final scene, the orchestra, assembled on stage, is ready at last to do its work, which, as Kuskin deftly sums things up for her readers, is "to play—beautifully."

When New York theater-page illustrator turned picture-book artist DON FREEMAN created *Pet of the Met* (1953) in collaboration with his wife, LYDIA, the **Metropolitan Opera Company** still occupied its original Victorian-era quarters at Broadway between 39th and 40th Streets. Glimpses of the grandly gilded, long-demolished house are preserved in the exuberant comic drawings of *Pet of the Met*, the Freemans' homage to the page-turners, prompters, and other unsung offstage heroes who help make the gloriously over-the-top opera world work.

In this sprightly tale, an ardent, music-loving mouse named Maestro Petrini plays a pivotal behind-the-scenes role during a children's matinee performance of Mozart's *The Magic Flute*. The Freemans had their own commitment to art-making for young audiences in mind, as well as the opera company's, when they wrote:

Pet of the Met,
by Don and Lydia Freeman

Just before the great golden curtains parted, the Prompter leaned over and whispered into his partner's [Maestro Petrini's] *ear, "We must be especially good today, my pet. Boys and girls deserve the very best you know!"*
—*Pet of the Met*

Since 1966 the Met has held forth from the stage of its new home at Lincoln Center, in the vast, arched-windowed hall located directly behind the fountain.

To the left of the fountain is the New York State Theater, home of the New York City Ballet. The early years of this company's first prima ballerina are recalled in *Tallchief*, by MARIA TALLCHIEF, with ROSEMARY WELLS, illustrated by GARY KELLEY (1999). For Lincoln Center tour information (including Avery Fisher Hall, the Metropolitan Opera House, and the New York State Theater): 212-875-5350; lincolncenter.org. The New York Public Library's **Library for the Performing Arts**, located just to the north of and behind the Met, offers free exhibitions and an impressive array of books and other materials of interest to children.

When you are ready to leave Lincoln Center, return to Columbus Avenue, walk north to 68th Street and turn right, pausing in front of **25 West 68th Street**, the Hatcher family home in Judy Blume's *Tales of a Fourth Grade Nothing* (1972) and *Double Fudge* (2002). Nine-year-old Peter Hatcher enjoys living here, even though it means having to share his busy parents with his troublesome, attention-grabbing preschooler brother, Fudge.

It's an old apartment building. But it's got one of the best elevators in New York City. There are mirrors all around.

You can see yourself from every angle. . . . Our apartment's on the twelfth floor. But I don't have to tell Henry [the elevator operator]. . . . He knows everybody in the building. . . . He even knows I'm nine and in the fourth grade.

—*Tales of a Fourth Grade Nothing*

It is here that the head of the Juicy-O juice company comes to dinner, with disastrous results for his advertising copywriter, Mr. Hatcher; that Fudge's third birthday party turns totally wild; and that Peter and his schoolmates plan their fourth-grade class project on "The City."

Walk east along West 68th Street and, turning left onto Central Park West, continue north. On crossing 71st Street, watch for the Majestic apartment house at **115 Central Park West**, home to Annabel Andrews in **Mary Rodgers**'s hilarious fantasy about role reversals gone haywire, *Freaky Friday* (1972).

The author—daughter of Broadway composer Richard Rodgers and writer Dorothy Rodgers—had already made a name for herself as the creator of the musical *Once Upon a Mattress* when she began writing children's books. From the opening lines, *Freaky Friday*, her second book, is uproarious, post-Freudian fun.

You are not going to believe me, nobody in their right minds could possibly believe me, but it's true, really it is!

When I woke up this morning, I found I'd turned into my mother. —*Freaky Friday*

Rodgers, without ever explaining just *how* the metamorphosis could have occurred, has readers eagerly following along as 13-year-old Annabel, who only a day earlier said she couldn't wait to be a grown-up, now learns more than she bargained for about being a parent. In the course of a single day spent in her mother's body, poor Annabel has to deal with unruly children, a broken washer, and an upsetting school conference (in which her own failings as a student are hashed out in excruciating detail). She even forgets to meet her "son's" (i.e., younger brother's) bus, a slipup that prompts this spluttery telephone call to the police:

"Officer Plonchik, do you by any chance happen to recall an incident that occurred at approximately twelve seventeen today on the corner of 71st and Central Park West, involving a darling little six-year-old boy whose mother was two minutes late meeting him at the school bus?"

"Yeah?" said Plonchik, by which he seemed to mean I should keep talking.

"Well, this is the mother speaking and I want to thank you very much for everything you did . . ."

—*Freaky Friday*

Rodgers brings it all off in a lighthearted spirit of farce, taking care to restore Annabel and her mom to their own bodies well before bedtime.

Continue north along Central Park West, stopping once you have crossed 77th Street. The massive castlelike structure now before you is the **American Museum of Natural History** (daily 10 A.M.–5:45 P.M.; Fri. to 8:45 P.M.; 212-769-5100; www.amnh.org). Holed up for a time in New York, Holden Caulfield, the disaffected teen in J.D. SALINGER's *The Catcher in the Rye* (1951), recalls with grudging fondness the frequent field trips his grade-school class once made to this great storehouse of scientific and ethnographic artifacts. Within a decade of its publication, Salinger's hard-hitting novel inspired the new genre of realistic young-adult fiction. Enter by the West 77th Street door (if in use). Otherwise, choose the Central Park West entrance and follow the signs down one flight to the West 77th Street lobby to see:

. . . This long, long Indian canoe, about as long as three goddam Cadillacs in a row, with about twenty Indians in it, some of them paddling, some of them just standing around looking rough, and they all had war paint all over their faces. There was one very spooky guy in the back of the canoe, with a mask on. He was the witch doctor. He gave me the creeps, but I liked him anyway. . . . Then, just before you went inside the auditorium, . . . you passed this Eskimo. He was sitting over a hole in this icy lake, and he was fishing through it. . . . The best thing, though, . . . was that every-

thing always stayed right where it was. Nobody'd move. You could go there a hundred thousand times, and that Eskimo would still be just finished catching those two fish. . . . The only thing that would be different would be you.

—The Catcher in the Rye

Still on view just beyond the museum's West 77th Street entrance, the boat described here is a 63-foot-long, nineteenth-century Haida canoe. Caulfield—and Salinger—were wrong about one thing, however. The Eskimo fisherman in the glass case is gone. As you walk past the canoe and through the Northwest Coast Indians Hall toward the museum's auditorium, you will instead pass life-size tableaux depicting a Tlingit potlatch ceremony and gatherings of Kwakiutl craftsmen.

JON SCIESZKA's *2095*, illustrated by LANE SMITH (1995), serves up a lighter and (to borrow one of this author's favorite words) goofier account of a class trip here. Nowhere in the museum will you find the time-travel rooms where Fred, Sam, and Joe—Scieszka's Time Warp Trio—experience robot-riddled life at the end of the twenty-first century. But Joe's checklist of other favorite American Museum of Natural History destinations amounts to a good sampling of the museum's incredibly rich and varied collections.

They've got a prehistoric alligator skull [look for "Knife-face," in the 4th-floor Vertebrate Origins gallery] that's bigger than you, a herd of charging stuffed elephants [2nd-floor Akeley Hall of African Mammals], and a car with a hole in it [alas, no longer on display in the nonetheless still fascinating 1st-floor Hall of Meteorites] from where it got bashed by a meteorite. If you sit close enough to the animal exhibits [various halls], it feels like you're right in the jungle or the mountain or the desert. And on hot summer days I like to go sit under the blue whale hanging from the ceiling in the ocean life room [1st floor, not far from the Haida canoe]. It's blue and quiet and cool. —2095

And yes, the museum gift shop *does* sell rubber ants.

Two excellent photobiographies describe the pioneering field research of one of the museum's first scientist-adventurers. *Secrets from the Rocks*, by ALBERT MARRIN (2002), and *Dragon Bones and Dinosaur Eggs*, by ANN BAUSUM (2000), complement each other with their vivid accounts of Roy Chapman Andrews and his team's discoveries during the 1920s of an extraordinary array of prehistoric fossil remains. To see some of their revelatory finds, go to the fourth-floor **Hall of Ornithischian Dinosaurs**. On display there: a diorama of Protoceratops (the first horned-face dinosaur); a "growth series" showing the development from hatchling to adult of a *Protoceratops Andrewski* skull; and a collection of the first dinosaur eggs known to science.

You could easily spend several days exploring this vast, atticlike museum. One author who did so as a boy is juvenile science writer SEYMOUR SIMON. Then as now, astronomy was Simon's greatest scientific passion. By the mid-1940s the teenaged future author of *The Universe* (1998) and over 200 other books, was president of the Hayden Planetarium's Junior Astronomy Club, with his own key to the museum. Now completely redesigned and contained within the **Rose Center for Earth and Space**, Simon's old haunt is a more spectacular site than ever for city stargazing.

On exiting the museum, return to West 77th Street and look across to the apartment house at **number 16**, home of the 11-year-old heroine of LULI GRAY's fantasy-adventure novel, *Falcon's Egg* (1995). Then gaze up at the **Astor Turret**, the Romanesque Revival tower that stands guard at the museum's southeast corner. A staff scientist with an office in this tower helps Emily Falcon Davies solve the mystery of the outsized egg she finds one day in Central Park. The gigantic egg is strangely hot to the touch. Stranger still, when it finally hatches out, the creature to emerge from it is neither a bird nor an ordinary reptile but a dragon.

Astor Turret, the American Museum of Natural History

Falcon stared out at the huge stone building across 77th Street. Her great-great-aunt Emily always said you could learn about almost anything at the museum. . . . "Ardene," Falcon said [to her neighbor], *"my aunt Emily, she knows someone there, a man who writes about birds, a . . . an . . . orthenologist, I think it is."*

"Ornithologist," said Ardene. "What's his name?"

"Freddy," said Falcon. "That's all I know, she calls him Freddy."
                                                      —*Falcon's Egg*

Falcon happens upon her fantastic discovery in the tall grass along the western edge of Central Park's **Great Lawn**. To get there, enter the park at West 77th, take the footpath north, and follow signs for the Delacorte Theater, to the right. Keep walking, and once you have taken in the grand expanse of the Great Lawn, which lies just beyond the theater, walk south (and around Turtle Pond) to the fanciful **Belvedere Castle**, the turreted stone structure that once served as the city's weather station. Climb the steps to the balcony, as Falcon does, for a commanding view of the Great Lawn and beyond.

WALKING TOUR II

We begin at the **Children's Museum of Manhattan** (212 West 83rd Street, between Amsterdam and Broadway; 212-721-1223; www.cmom.org). Take the 1 or 9 train to the 86th Street stop. In addition to the interactive exhibits and family activities offered here, this lively museum has become one of the best places in New York for viewing original art from children's books. In recent years, exhibitions have featured the work of Ezra Jack Keats, H.A. Rey, Ed Young, and David Wiesner.

Now walk (or take the Number 104 bus) north on Broadway to West 111th Street. The title character of VIRGINIA HAMILTON's stormed-tossed novel, *The Planet of Junior Brown* (1971), loves this wide avenue with its "concrete islands," tempting bakery smells, and "different faces . . . passing him."

Growing up in the Bronx during the 1940s, JOHANNA HURWITZ read voraciously and dreamed of becoming a children's book author and librarian. Of all the books she read as a child, the ones that were to have the greatest influence on her own work were the Betsy-Tacy series of historical novels by Maud Hart Lovelace. At first, young Johanna concluded that to follow properly in her role model's example, she would need to write stories set in the author's native state of Minnesota, even though she had never been to Minnesota herself. She later realized that to write "like" Lovelace could also mean to write about the place *she* knew best—New York City.

Hurwitz set **Busybody Nora** (1976) and several later chapter books about Nora, Teddy, Russell, Elisa, and Marshall in the apartment house at **532 West 111th Street**, between Broadway and Amsterdam Avenue. The author herself lived in this building at the time she wrote the first of her gently humorous tales of friendship and family life as seen from a young child's perspective. In *Busybody Nora*, for instance, Hurwitz has us view Nora's building as the 5½-year-old heroine sees it.

> *She liked to imagine the other people in the building. It was funny to think about 199 other people all brushing their teeth at the same time. Or 199 other people all putting slices of bread in their toasters. Or 199 other people turning out the light to go to sleep. . . . Yet even though they lived in the same building, and she had lived there all her life, . . . Nora hadn't seen all the people.* —Busybody Nora

One block north, the contemporary reddish brown brick building on the southwest corner of Broadway and West 112th Street is the **Bank Street College of Education** (212-875-4400; www.bnkst.edu).

Named for its original headquarters at 69 Bank Street in Greenwich Village [see p. 25], this vibrant institution combines an innovative private school (pre-school through eighth grade) with a world-renowned teacher-training program and research center focused on the full range of children's educational needs. A plaque honoring

Bank Street alumna Margaret Wise Brown, "author of *Goodnight Moon* and *The Runaway Bunny*," can be seen on the wall just to the left of the main entrance.

Now walk east along West 112th Street, crossing Amsterdam Avenue. Before you stands the Episcopal **Cathedral of St. John the Divine**, the world's largest cathedral. Tour information: 212-316-7540; www.stjohn divine.org.

Cathedral of St. John the Divine

In *Cutters, Carvers & the Cathedral* (1995), photographer GEORGE ANCONA documents the ongoing construction of this beloved house of worship and community center, and describes an innovative apprenticeship program that, during the 1990s, introduced neighborhood teens to the stonemason's craft.

St. John the Divine is also a principal setting of MADELEINE L'ENGLE's darkly nuanced novel of suspense, *The Young Unicorns* (1968).

Written at a time of widespread urban unrest and mistrust of institutional authority, *The Young Unicorns* examines the entwined lives of a small group of young Upper West Siders and the adults closest to them, including powerful clerics associated with the cathedral. A web of intrigue spreads to involve young and old alike in a test of wits and wills, with the fate of the city itself hanging in the balance.

L'Engle's close knowledge of the cathedral (she served for many years as its writer-in-residence) is evident in her evocative descriptions of its soaring main sanctuary and honeycomb of side chapels.

Dave moved through the music [coming from the cathedral organ] down the nave and up the steps to the ambulatory. St. James Chapel lay ahead of him, dark now, settling into the shadows for the night. Bishop Potter's great white marble sarcophagus caught a pale glimmer of light; the cross above the altar at the crossing glinted gold. Dave looked along the dim crescent of the ambulatory, past St. James, around towards St. Ambrose, St. Martin of Tours, St. Saviour, St. Columba, St. Boniface, St. Ansgar . . .

—*The Young Unicorns*

L'Engle fans will recognize the Austin family from the author's **Meet the Austins** (1960), **A Ring of Endless Light** (1980), and other novels. In *The Young Unicorns*, we find them living upstairs from the Gregorys, whose daughter Emily has become their friend. The Gregory family house is modeled on **River Mansion**, located on the south side of West 106th Street, at the corner of Riverside Drive. The abandoned subway station described in *The Young Unicorns* is one of several such "ghosts" to be found in New York; the station referred to is at West 96th Street along the Number 1 IRT line. You can glimpse this graffiti-covered phantom by riding the Number 1 north from West 86th Street or south from West 96th.

HARLEM ■ NORTHERN MANHATTAN

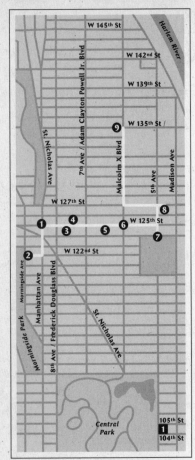

HARLEM

■

NORTHERN MANHATTAN

*O*riginally named "Nieuw Haarlem," after the Dutch city of Haarlem, by colonial governor Peter Stuyvesant, this large portion of northern Manhattan was first developed as farmland, with a thriving village at present-day East 125th Street along the Harlem River. The first African Americans to live in Harlem came as Dutch farmers' slaves.

The construction of the New York and Harlem Railroad in 1837, and later in the 1800s of elevated train lines, spurred urbanization. By the 1890s, Harlem boasted some of the city's most elegant row-house neighborhoods as well as a large stock of middle-class housing. Harlem's population at this time was predominantly German.

As blocks of affordable housing went up around the turn of the last century, many eastern European Jews left the Lower East Side for this part of town. For the first time, large numbers of African-American New Yorkers also moved here, seeking better living conditions and a haven from racial discrimination experienced elsewhere around the city. During the 1920s and 1930s, the "Great Migration" of southern blacks to northern cities further enlarged the area's African-American population; this period culminated in the creative flowering of the "Harlem Renaissance" in literature, music, and art. At the same time, a portion of East Harlem became a magnet for northward-bound, job-seeking Puerto Rican Americans. Their arrival marked the beginnings of today's Spanish Harlem, or *El Barrio*. After World War II, Harlem as a whole remained in an economic decline that had its origins in the Great Depression of the 1930s. By the 1960s, outsiders pointed to the area as a symbol of urban poverty and decay. Far from resigned to their problems, however, the Harlem community played an historic role in the civil-rights movement of the 1950s and 1960s. As the twenty-first century began, this section of Manhattan stood poised on the threshold of a broadly based new economic as well as cultural renaissance.

WALKING   TOUR   I

We begin our tour at the corner of West 125th Street (now also known as Martin Luther King Jr. Boulevard) and St. Nicholas Avenue, by the subway station that Duke Ellington, in his immortal swing anthem "Take the A Train," recommended as the best way to travel to this part of town. *Duke Ellington*, by ANDREA DAVIS PINKNEY, illustrated by BRIAN PINKNEY (1998), introduces young readers to the life and times of the great American musician and composer.

Walk south from this major intersection along St. Nicholas for one block, then bearing right onto Manhattan Avenue, continue for two more blocks. Turning right onto West 122nd Street, walk one block to the Presbyterian **Church of the Master**. Although the original brick structure is boarded up for future renovation, it is still worth seeing. It was here that WALTER DEAN MYERS, the novelist, poet, and nonfiction writer who has written more for young people about Harlem life than anyone in the last quarter century, spent much of his childhood. As Myers recalls in his memoir *Bad Boy* (2001):

> *In Bible school, which I attended summers at the Church of the Master, I had learned to weave a lanyard out of plastic strips. There was a clip at the end of the lanyard, and onto this I hooked the key ring. Almost all the kids in the neighborhood with working parents had their keys around their necks on either strings or plastic key chains made in Bible school.* —Bad Boy

Now retrace your steps to West 125th Street and walk west past the Harlem USA shopping mall, developed by ex-basketball superstar Magic Johnson. On this block, at what was once **number 306**, artist ROMARE BEARDEN opened his first studio in the 1930s. The studio soon became a meeting place for fellow artists and writers including Jacob Lawrence, Norman Lewis, Ernest Chichlow, Claude McKay, and Langston Hughes.

In 1971, Bearden created a large, six-panel mixed-media collage called "The Block" as an homage to the vitality of Harlem community life. Intended as a distillation rather than as a documentary portrait of a specific street scene, this energetic work can be viewed up close in the extraordinary picture book named for it. In **The Block** (1995), Bearden's collage is reproduced in full, then divided into sections, each of which is paired, evocatively, with a poem by LANGSTON HUGHES. As an informal companion to *The Block*, read Walter Dean Myers's **145th Street** (2000), a collection of short stories set on and around the block-long stretch of West 145th Street between Adam Clayton Powell and Malcolm X Boulevards.

Apollo Theater

Cross West 125th Street and, also crossing Eighth Avenue, continue on to the famed **Apollo Theater** (253 West 125th Street, between Seventh and Eighth Avenues). In 1934 this former vaudeville house began its run as Harlem's premier showcase for musical talent. The roster of performers who have appeared here includes Count Basie, Billie Holiday, Nat "King" Cole, Lionel Hampton, Stevie Wonder, Smokey Robinson, and the Jackson Five. *Uptown* (2000), collage artist BRYAN COLLIER's picture-book paean

Uptown, *by Bryan Collier*

to Harlem, features a view of the familiar marquee head-lining the Boys Choir of Harlem and Apollo Amateur Night, a Wednesday evening ritual since 1935. CHARLES R. SMITH JR. combines photographs and poetry in his affectionate tribute to the Boys Choir, *Perfect Harmony* (2002).

Continue east one more block and cross West 125th Street to visit the **Studio Museum in Harlem** (144 West 125th Street; 212-864-4500; www.studiomuseuminharlem.org). This vital gallery space presents changing exhibitions that celebrate African-American creativity in the arts. The museum is open, free of charge, for special family activities on the first Saturday of every month.

Among the many artists whose work has been shown at the Studio Museum is JACOB LAWRENCE, the print-maker and painter who came of age in Harlem alongside Romare Bearden and Langston Hughes. During 1940–1941, Lawrence created the series of sixty paintings reproduced in a memorable picture book, *The Great Migration: An American Story* (1993). These stylized yet powerfully direct images chronicle the major population shift that, during the 1920s and 1930s, brought millions of African-Americans (including the artist's own family) north in search of a better life. Lawrence's emergence from humble beginnings to become one of America's most revered artists is recounted for young people in *Story Painter: The Life of Jacob Lawrence*, by JOHN DUGGLEBY (1998).

Continue east along 125th Street to the end of the block. Before crossing Malcolm X Boulevard, note the entrance to the **125th Street Station of the IRT subway**. This station is well worth a visit as the platform walls on both the uptown and downtown sides are decorated with spectacular ceramic mosaic murals by artist and picture-book author FAITH RINGGOLD. The title of Ringgold's Caldecott Honor book (and first children's book) *Tar Beach* (1991) recalls a local term for the tar-covered tenement rooftops where Harlem residents have traditionally gathered on summer evenings in search of relief from the heat. In this lyrical story based on the

I could see our tiny rooftop, with Mommy and Daddy and Mr. and Mrs. Honey, our next-door neighbors, still playing cards as if nothing was going on,

and Be Be, my baby brother, lying real still on the mattress, just like I told him to, his eyes like huge floodlights tracking me through the sky.

Tar Beach, *by Faith Ringgold*

artist's childhood, young Cassie Louise Lightfoot is lifted by the stars from her rooftop perch and soars over the city's streets and the bejeweled George Washington Bridge, claiming them all for herself. Images of flight have deep roots in the African-American lore associated with the longing for freedom from slavery and oppression. Ringgold's subway murals, titled *Flying Home: Harlem Heroes and Heroines* (1996), return to this powerful theme. Consider choosing this station as your point of departure following the tour.

Now walk east one additional long block along West 125th Street to Fifth Avenue. Turn right onto Fifth and walk one block south to **Marcus Garvey Memorial Park**, a green space named for the charismatic organizer of the post–World War I Back to Africa movement. MARY LAWLER tells the story of Garvey's battle for black rights in *Marcus Garvey: Black Nationalist Leader* (1988). Look for the city's last remaining fire watchtower, built on high ground here in 1856.

When you are ready to leave the park, walk north for three blocks on Fifth to East 127th Street and turn right onto Langston Hughes Place, stopping at 20 East 127th, the **Langston Hughes House**. Harlem's poet laureate lived here from 1947 until his death twenty years later. Tours are by appointment. For information: 212-280-7888; www.harlemheritage.com.

Langston Hughes's bittersweet blues-inspired lyrics

have earned him a place among America's greatest poets. A less well-known side of his work consists of the handful of books he wrote expressly for children, including a poetry collection, *The Dream Keeper and Other Poems* (1932), re-illustrated by Brian Pinkney (1994). *Black Misery*, illustrated by AROUNI (1969), is a book of aphorisms in which Hughes gives his pointed response to white America's sentimentalization of childhood, as exemplified by Joan Walsh Anglund's *Love Is a Special Way of Feeling* (1960). "Misery," writes Hughes, "is when you heard on the radio that the neighborhood you live in is a slum but you always thought it was home."

Hughes's *The Sweet and Sour Animal Book* (1994) has special Harlem associations. The witty rhymes —one for every alphabet letter from *A* to *Z*, each describing a different animal—were discovered among Hughes's unpublished papers at Yale and shown to young students at the dynamic **Harlem School of the Arts** (645 St. Nicholas Avenue). The children created three-dimensional artworks inspired by the poems. Photographs of their spirited sculptures appear side by side with Hughes's poetry in this vibrant picture book.

Three other picture books offer glimpses of Hughes and his world. Bryan Collier's lushly textured expressionistic collages in *Visiting Langston*, text by WILLIE PERDOMO (2002), follow a young girl and her father as they tour the Hughes house. TONY MEDINA recounts Hughes's life story in a sequence of brief first-person poems in *Love to Langston*, illustrated

Love to Langston, *by Tony Medina, illustrated by R. Gregory Christie*

by R. GREGORY CHRISTIE (2002). In *Langston Hughes: American Poet*, illustrated by CATHERINE DEETER (2001), novelist ALICE WALKER sketches Hughes's biography in prose and recalls the day when, as an aspiring young writer, she visited him at his East 127th Street home.

Return to Malcolm X Boulevard and head north eight blocks to the **Schomburg Center for Research in Black Culture** (515 Malcolm X Blvd., corner West 135th Street; 212-491-2200; www.schomburgcenter.org). This major research division of the New York Public Library is named for the Puerto Rican–born, African-American scholar Arturo Alfonso Schomburg, whose private collection of books, art objects, and artifacts forms the core of the center's treasures. The Schomburg, with extensive holdings of manuscripts, photographs, prints and paintings, films, and sound recordings, is perhaps the best place in the United States to learn more about the cultural achievements of the Harlem Renaissance. Two excellent introductions to the subject are JIM HASKINS's history, *The Harlem Renaissance* (1996), and NIKKI GIOVANNI's poetry anthology with commentary, *Shimmy Shimmy Shimmy Like My Sister Kate* (1996). (NOTE: To see Faith Ringgold's subway mosaics, consider taking the uptown Number 2 or 3 train one stop from 125th Street to the Schomburg Center; then, on leaving the Center, take the downtown Number 2 or 3 train one stop to 125th Street to view the mosaic on that side of the platform.)

More Harlem Books

The Contender, by ROBERT LIPSYTE (1967), charts a Harlem teen's quest for dignity in and out of the boxing ring, under the tutelage of a veteran trainer modeled on the legendary Cus D'Amato.

Dave at Night, by GAIL CARSON LEVINE (1999). In this Dickensian glimpse of 1920s uptown Manhattan, an 11-year-old Jewish orphan sneaks out nights from the grim Hebrew Home for Boys, located somewhere in Harlem, and, together with the new friends he makes on his nocturnal rounds, experiences the heady, after-hours world of the Harlem Renaissance.

The Friends, by ROSA GUY (1973), and its two sequels, *Ruby* (1976) and *Edith Jackson* (1978), follow the struggles for survival, acceptance, and love of two West Indian–born teenage sisters who come to Harlem to join their parents.

The Harlem Nutcracker, by DONALD BYRD, photographed by SUSAN KUKLIN (2001), is a re-imagining of the traditional Christmas ballet as a story set in a lush Harlem mansion of the 1920s. Kuklin's photographs document a performance of this provocative work. The accompanying narrative is by the choreographer who created it.

Me and Uncle Romie, by CLAIRE HARTFIELD, illustrated by JEROME LAGARRIGUE (2002), describes, in fictional form, a North Carolina child's heady introductory visit to artist Romare Bearden's Harlem studio and world.

Monster, by WALTER DEAN MYERS, illustrated by CHRISTOPHER MYERS (1999), is a riveting chronicle, cast in part as a screenplay, of the trial of a 16-year-old accused of participation in a Harlem convenience-store robbery gone murderously sour. The Myerses' *Harlem* (1997)—Christopher is Walter's son—is the team's soaring tribute in verse and mixed-media collage art to the neighborhood. Among Walter Dean Myers's many earlier novels is the now classic *Scorpions* (1988), in which a decent kid gets caught up in tragic events amid the gang violence of the Harlem streets. Myers is also the author of two biographies of Malcolm X, the controversial African-American leader who lived and died in Harlem—for younger children, *Malcolm X: A Fire Burning Brightly*, illustrated by LEONARD JENKINS (2000), and for older readers, *Malcolm X: By Any Means Necessary* (1993).

El Barrio (Spanish Harlem)

To learn more about this portion of Harlem, which lies between Third and Fifth Avenues, from East 120th Street south to East 96th Street, start with a visit to **El Museo del Barrio**, 1230 Fifth Avenue at 104th Street (Wed.– Sun.: 11 A.M.–5 P.M.; 212-831-7272; www.elmuseo.org). To get there, take the Number 6 Lexington Avenue subway line to the East 103rd Street station; walk two blocks west to Fifth Avenue and one block north to 104th Street.

Founded by Puerto Rican community activists in 1969, this museum has expanded its mission to become a center for the celebration and study of Puerto Rican, Caribbean, and Latin American culture, art, and community life. Family events and programs are scheduled throughout the year.

These are some of the best books for young people about life in this part of New York:

Eddy's Dream, by MIRIAM COHEN, photographed by ADAM COHEN (2000), evokes a lonely East Harlem immigrant child's longing to visit Puerto Rico and his grandmother again.

Grandma's Records, by ERIC VELASQUEZ (2001), tells the story of a boy's summer sojourn in New York's *El Barrio*. Thanks to his grandmother's knowledge and enthusiasm, the young visitor discovers the music and cultural heritage of his Puerto Rican homeland.

Nilda, by NICHOLASA MOHR (1973), is a no-punches-pulled novel about growing up young, talented, female, and Puerto Rican in New York's rough-and-tumble *El Barrio* at the time of World War II. The author's own family lived on East 100th Street between Madison and Park Avenues during those same years. Mohr's *Felita* (1979) describes the hostile reception with which her family was greeted when they later moved to a predominantly white neighborhood just a few blocks east of *El Barrio*.

A Visit to the Little Red Lighthouse

Take the A train to the 181st Street station, and from the corner of Fort Washington Avenue and West 181st

Street, walk three blocks west to where 181st Street ends, at Riverside Drive. Turn right onto Riverside and look for the footbridge over the West Side Highway. On crossing the bridge, take the path to the left, leading into the wooded area of Fort Washington Park. This winding, downward-sloping walkway will bring you to the **Little Red Lighthouse**—and a lawn that is perfect for picnics.

The Little Red Lighthouse and the George Washington Bridge

Built in 1880 and commissioned at its present site by the United States Coast Guard in 1921, this modest lighthouse guided mariners along the river until 1932, when the government deactivated it following the construction of the George Washington Bridge. It seemed marked for oblivion when, in 1942, *The Little Red Lighthouse and the Great Gray Bridge*, a picture book by HILDEGARDE H. SWIFT, illustrated by LYND WARD, immortalized the diminutive, tomato-red iron and steel tower as a universal symbol of the enduring value of small but dependable things. Such was the popularity of the fable that when the Coast Guard proposed in 1951 to demolish the lighthouse, a public outcry (led by protesting children and *The New York Times*) halted the plan. Responsibility for the structure was transferred to the New York City Department of Parks and Recre-

The Little Red Lighthouse and the Great Gray Bridge, *by Hildegarde H. Swift, illustrated by Lynd Ward*

ation, which continues to maintain the Little Red Lighthouse today.

Lighthouse tours can be arranged throughout the year
by calling Urban Park Rangers at 212-304-2365. The
very best time to visit, however, is during the annual Little Red Lighthouse Festival, which is usually held on a
Saturday in mid- to late-September. Festival goers are
treated to hayrides, musical performances, environmental
exhibits, and a celebrity reading of the children's book
that saved the day for this New York landmark. For festival information, call the Historic House Trust of New
York City: 212-360-8203; www.preserve.org.

BROOKLYN

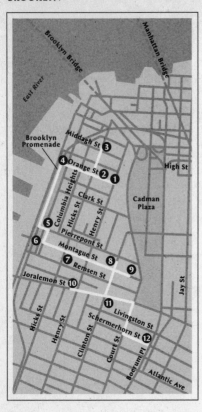

◀ Walking Tour I

❶ Corner of Henry & Orange St.

❷ Plymouth Church of the Pilgrims

❸ P.S. 8 (37 Hicks St.)

❹ Brooklyn Promenade (Esplanade)

❺ Pierrepont Street Playground

❻ Flagpole and plaque marking Washington's headquarters

❼ Hotel Bossert (98 Montague St.)

❽ Brooklyn Historical Society (128 Pierrepont St.)

❾ Former Brooklyn Dodgers Baseball Club headquarters (211 Montague St.)

❿ 105 Joralemon St. (home of Tucker Woolf)

⓫ Packer Collegiate Institute (170 Joralemon St.)

⓬ New York Transit Museum

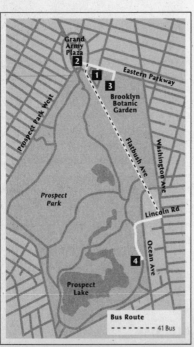

◀ Walking Tour II / Excursion

❶ Ingersoll Memorial Library, Brooklyn Public Library / Youth Wing

❷ Soldiers' and Sailors' Memorial Arch

❸ Brooklyn Botanic Garden / Celebrity Path

❹ Prospect Park / Imagination Playground

BROOKLYN

WALKING   TOUR   I
Brooklyn Heights

Our tour of New York's most populous borough begins with one of its oldest neighborhoods, Brooklyn Heights.

Located just across the East River from Wall Street, Brooklyn Heights was New York City's first suburb. Dutch settlers farmed here in the seventeenth century. After Robert Fulton established his steam-powered ferry service in 1814, prosperous Manhattan merchants began to build elegant homes in what soon became known as a neighborhood of tree-shaded streets and stately churches. The commute from Fulton Ferry Landing, just down the hill from "the Heights," to Manhattan's South Street Landing took less than ten minutes. Poet and Brooklyn newspaperman Walt Whitman made the trip often and immortalized the experience in his poem "Crossing Brooklyn Ferry" (1856).

The opening of the Brooklyn Bridge in 1883, and of the first subway link to the neighborhood (the IRT) in 1908, further spurred the neighborhood's growth and prosperity. After 1898, when Brooklyn gave up its independent status to join the newly consolidated City of New York, Manhattan became the undisputed focus of high-rise construction. Perhaps for this reason, Brooklyn Heights's unrivaled collection of three- and four-story pre–Civil War buildings largely escaped the wrecking ball. Artists and writers discovered the neighborhood in the 1940s and 1950s, a time when local real-estate prices were in temporary decline. In 1965, the neighborhood as a whole was designated the city's first historic district and national landmark.

Our tour of this atmospheric, child-friendly part of town begins at the corner of Henry and Orange Streets,

Henry Ward Beecher,
by Gutzon Borglum

one block from both the High Street/ Brooklyn Bridge stop on the A and C subway lines and the Clark Street stop on the Number 2 and 3 trains. As you walk along Orange Street, which begins at this intersection, watch on your right for the grouping of stately old brick buildings and gardens that comprise **Plymouth Church of the Pilgrims**, where, for forty years, famed nineteenth-century orator and abolitionist Reverend Henry Ward Beecher held forth. Under his impassioned leadership, this church became known as the "Grand Central Depot" of the Underground Railroad. As WILLIAM LOREN KATZ notes in *Black Legacy: A History of New York's African Americans* (1997), Plymouth once also served as the setting of a widely publicized mock slave auction, conducted by Beecher himself in an effort to dramatize the inhumanity of slavery. The garden statue (by Gutzon Borglum, 1914) catches the flamboyant clergyman in a characteristic pose.

Continue along Orange Street to the end of the block, turn right onto Hicks Street, and walk two blocks to Middagh Street, where you will come to **P.S. 8**, the school attended by the Chinese immigrant girl heroine of BETTE BAO LORD's poignant autobiographical novel, set in 1947, called *In the Year of the Boar and Jackie Robinson*, illustrated by MARC SIMONT (1984) (see also p. 104).

P.S. 8, Brooklyn Heights

Now return to Orange Street and continue for two more blocks. Crossing Columbia Heights, descend the pedestrian ramp to the **Brooklyn Promenade** (officially, the "Esplanade"), the nearly one-third-mile-long scenic walkway that has been dazzling strollers with its harbor views since 1951.

Author-artist DONALD CREWS lived in Brooklyn at the time he created *Harbor* (1982), a now-classic picture book about the boats and ships that ply the city's waters. Not surprisingly, Crews chose to depict New York Harbor from a Brooklynite's perspective. Allowing for artistic license, the

Brooklyn Promenade

views of the Manhattan skyline seen in this book's colorful pages are those visible from the Promenade and from

Harbor, *by Donald Crews*

farther to the north and south along the East River's Brooklyn shoreline. The low-slung sky-blue warehouses pictured in some illustrations are those lining the waterfront below the Heights. From the yam-colored Staten Island Ferry to the spray-crowned city fireboat that furnishes this picture book's spectacular finale, the boat and ship types depicted in *Harbor* can all be found in the waters around New York today.

One of the most remarkable things about the Promenade is the sheer number of New York landmarks that can be glimpsed from this single vantage point: the Statue of Liberty, Ellis Island, the Empire State and Chrysler Buildings, and, closest at hand, the Brooklyn Bridge. This was also one of the best places to see the upper reaches of the World Trade Center's Twin Towers. In the hours and days following the terrorist attacks of September 11, 2001, the Promenade became one of the principal shrines where New Yorkers gathered to talk, bring flowers, light candles, and post photos of the missing.

Brooklyn Bridge by LYNN CURLEE (2001) tells the stirring tale of engineering prowess, civic pride, and personal courage that resulted in the monumental structure that contemporary New Yorkers hailed as the "Eighth Wonder of the World." Built between 1867 and 1883, the graceful suspension bridge with its massive Gothic tow-

ers and spiderweb cable construction was the creation of German-born engineer John A. Roebling. After Roebling's death in 1869, his son, Washington, and daughter-in-law, Emily, took charge of the project. The Roeblings lived in a row house (since demolished) at 106 Columbia Heights, where, from an upstairs window and with

Brooklyn Bridge, *by Lynn Curlee*

the aid of a telescope, they supervised the complex and often dangerous construction work.

Walking south along the Promenade, pause to notice (and perhaps to visit) the **Pierrepont Street Playground**, one of many neighborhood locales pictured in *A Teeny Tiny Baby*, by AMY SCHWARTZ (1994).

Chances are you will want to continue walking to the Promenade's southern endpoint, at Remsen Street (two blocks past Pierrepont). To continue the tour, double back the equivalent of one city block to the Montague Street exit, noting as you go the **flagpole and plaque** marking the location of General George Washington's August 1776 headquarters, at the time of the Continental army's defeat in the Battle of Brooklyn.

As you walk east along Montague Street, the neighborhood's main shopping and dining corridor, stop to notice the lovingly restored **Hotel Bossert**, at 98 Montague Street and the corner of Hicks. Now owned by the Jehovah's Witnesses and off-limits to nonchurch members, the Bossert was the birthplace of picture-book author-illustrator BARBARA COONEY, whose grandfather, Louis

Bossert, built the once-luxurious hotel in 1909. The future two-time Caldecott Medal winner spent her first years living in the hotel's penthouse apartment, with views of the East River and beyond.

Louis Bossert was a prosperous mill-work manufacturer who first settled in the Bushwick section of Brooklyn. Cooney paid tribute to him and to all her Brooklyn forebears in *Hattie and the Wild Waves* (1990). The story is told in the voice of Mae Bossert, the author's mother, who recalls Louis saying: *" 'If*

Hotel Bossert

only there were a nice hotel in Brooklyn.' . . . And since there wasn't, he built one."

Continue along Montague Street for two blocks, turn-

Hattie and the Wild Waves,
by Barbara Cooney

ing left onto Clinton Street, and walk one block to the **Brooklyn Historical Society** (128 Pierrepont Street). This newly renovated museum and library houses thousands of artifacts and images from Brooklyn's past. Changing exhibitions and family activities highlight many of the same aspects of the borough's diverse cultural history as are featured in the books recommended in this tour.

Returning to Montague Street, walk left one block, stopping to read the bronze plaque on the building at 211 Montague Street, the former site of the **Brooklyn Dodgers Baseball Club headquarters**. It was here that on August 28, 1945, Jackie Robinson met with Dodgers owner Branch Rickey and agreed to join the team, thus becoming the first African-American player in the modern major leagues, following decades of segregation in professional baseball.

Several books for young people tell Robinson's powerful story. *Teammates*, by PETER GOLENBOCK, illustrated by PAUL BACON, with supplementary archival photographs (1990), makes plain the courage required by Robinson, as well as by Rickey, to overcome the game's legacy of racial discrimination. The climax of Golenbock's story comes with fellow Dodger Pee Wee Reese's public embrace of Robinson, a gesture that stunned and and profoundly influenced the attitudes of fans.

For older readers, *First in the Field*, by DEREK T. DINGLE (1998), provides a somewhat fuller biography and a more ample selection of archival photographs. Bette Bao Lord's novel *In the Year of the Boar and Jackie Robinson* suggests the enormous symbolic importance that Robinson's career had for Americans of all minorities. Lord's heroine, a newly arrived Chinese girl, listens in awe as her teacher describes the difficulties the Dodger first baseman had to overcome.

> *"Jackie Robinson is the grandson of a slave, the son of a sharecropper, raised in poverty by a lone mother . . . And now, Jackie Robinson is at bat in the big leagues."*
> *Suddenly Shirley understood why her father had brought her ten thousand miles to live among strangers. Here, she did not have to wait for gray hairs to be considered wise. . . . Here, Shirley Temple Wong was somebody. She felt as if she had the power of ten tigers, as if she had grown as tall as the Statue of Liberty.*
> —*In the Year of the Boar and Jackie Robinson*

Baseball fans will want to take the F train to its last stop (Coney Island station), in Coney Island, Brooklyn, and visit the permanent **Brooklyn Baseball Gallery** at **Keyspan Park** (1904 Surf Avenue, between West 17th and West 19th Streets; 718-449-8497).

Retrace your steps to Clinton Street. Turn left on Clinton and continue two blocks to Joralemon Street. One and a half blocks to the right, at **105 Joralemon**, is the home of Tucker Woolf, loyal friend of the title character of **M.E. KERR's** *Dinky Hocker Shoots Smack!* (1972). No, Dinky (aka Susan) does not *really* take hard drugs; she simply says she does in order to embarrass the heck out of her overbearing mother.

Returning to the corner of Clinton and Joralemon, cross Clinton and pause in front of the **Packer Collegiate Institute**, the large, castlelike brownstone structure at number 170 Joralemon. This is the school, pictured in Barbara Cooney's *Hattie and the Wild Waves*, where Mae Bossert studied as a girl. Four Bosserts attended Packer in all, as did an impressive roster of children's-book luminaries: MARY ALSOP O'HARA (author of *My Friend Flicka*), LOUISE SEAMAN BECHTEL (publish-

Packer Collegiate Institute

ing pioneer), RUTH SAWYER (Newbery winner for *Roller Skates*), HELEN SEWELL (original illustrator of LAURA INGALLS WILDER's *"Little House"* books), and LOIS LOWRY (Newbery medalist for both *Number the Stars* and *The Giver*).

More Brooklyn Artists and Writers Over the Years

ESTHER AVERILL • AVI • LLOYD BLOOM • PAT CUMMINGS • BRUCE DEGEN • DIANE AND LEO DILLON • PAULA FOX • MELANIE HOPE GREENBERG • JAMES HOWE • STEPHEN T. JOHNSON • KARLA KUSKIN • TED AND BETSY LEWIN • JANET MCDONALD • RICHARD MICHELSON • ALICE AND MARTIN PROVENSEN • JON SCIESZKA • BRIAN SELZNICK • MARILYN SINGER • JAVAKA STEPTOE • JOHN STEPTOE

Continue past Packer and turn right on Court Street. Walk two blocks, then cross Court at Schermerhorn Street and follow Schermerhorn to the end of the block and the entrance to the **New York Transit Museum** (corner of Schermerhorn and Boerum Place; 718-694-5100; www.mta.info/museum) located, appropriately, underground in an out-of-service 1930s subway station. Here you will find one of the world's great collections of period subway and elevated-train cars (nearly all of which are open to visitors), antique turnstiles, a working signal tower, and other mass-transit memorabilia.

It was true she [Rachel] had a number of ideas about New York before she got there which came in for quite a reshuffling when she saw how things really were. For instance, she had expected the elevated railway to be a little train running on narrow tracks from pole to pole about a half a mile in the air, really elevated. A sky train, she had thought, reached perhaps by ladder. . . . The subway, too, was not as she had expected. She had thought a subway would be a shining thing way way down in the middle of the earth. But there, she had merely to go down a flight of stairs . . .
—*Ginger Pye*, by ELEANOR ESTES

The museum also has an extensive collection of model buses and trains, special exhibits, weekend craft activities for families, and a friendly, knowledgeable staff.

Subway Sampler

Friday's Journey, by KEN RUSH (1994). In this affecting picture book, a 7-year-old whose parents are divorced shuttles by subway between his two homes and imagines himself to be in charge of the train, with the power to make it go anywhere.

Mim's Christmas Jam, by ANDREA DAVIS PINKNEY; illustrated by BRIAN PINKNEY (2001). An African-American family living in rural Pennsylvania in 1915 prepare to celebrate Christmas without the children's Pap, who has taken a job up north helping to build the New York City subway system.

Slake's Limbo, by FELICE HOLMAN (1974). Lonely, uncared-for 13-year-old Artemis Slake takes to the New

York subways in search of escape, finds a long-forgotten room of sorts deep in the subway tunnels under Grand Central Terminal, and decides to call it home.

Grand Army Plaza / Prospect Park

We begin our tour at the **Ingersoll Memorial Library**, the central building of the **Brooklyn Public Library** (southeast corner of Eastern Parkway and Flatbush Avenue; 718-230-2117; www.brooklynpubliclibrary.org), which is located one long block south of the Grand Army Plaza station of the Number 2 and 3 trains. Around the turn of the last century, this library, like the New York Public Library, served as a national model for library service to children. Brooklyn's influential first superintendent of work with children, Clara W. Hunt, played a key role in the creation of the Newbery Medal. The 1941 landmark structure and the nearby **Soldiers' and Sailors' Memorial Arch**, honoring the Union forces who fought in the Civil War, share a page in *Brooklyn Pops Up* by PAMELA THOMAS (2000). This witty pop-up and lift-the-flap guide to the borough's high spots features paper tableaux designed by MAURICE SENDAK, ROBERT SABUDA, DAVID A. CARTER, and others. It was originally published in conjunction with an exhibition of movable books presented at the library.

Walk along the library's Eastern Parkway side to the entrance of the completely refurbished **Youth Wing**. A special feature of this excellent lending and reference center for children and teens is the selection of quotations by favorite authors and illustrators—Brooklyn-born Maurice Sendak and EZRA JACK KEATS, among others—arrayed along the reading-room balcony wall.

Exit onto Eastern Parkway and continue east to the entrance to the **Brooklyn Botanic Garden** (718-623-7200; www.bbg.org). A visit here is a good idea at any time of the year. If you come in April, however, you will probably see the formal lawn just beyond the entrance as it is depicted in AMY SCHWARTZ's *A Teeny Tiny Baby*. The family of the baby in question have just encountered one of the garden guards. Having exchanged greetings with the visitors and learned that the baby is all of two weeks old, the graying uniformed gentleman remarks: "Ahhh, and already he's seen the forsythia."

Continue to the end of the lawn and turn left, following the path that leads straight ahead, then curves to the right. Of course, you may well want to stop at any number of the special plantings along the way. Once past the entrance to the Japanese Garden, however, watch on the right for the beginning of the **Celebrity Path**, a trail of stepping-stones, each bearing the name of a famous Brooklynite. As you walk this path, be on the lookout for the names of at least four children's-book authors and artists—Maurice Sendak and JOHN STEPTOE among them—in an honor roll that also includes Arthur Miller, Mae West, Mary Tyler Moore, and Harry Houdini.

A Teeny Tiny Baby, *by Amy Schwartz*

When you are ready to leave the garden, return to the Eastern Parkway gate. On Labor Day each year, Eastern Parkway, from Grand Army Plaza to Utica Avenue, is the scene of New York's largest parade and street fair—the West Indian–American Day Carnival. For information about this over-the-top spectacle, consult: www.carnaval. com/cityguides/newyork/ny_carn.htm. A picture book that captures the excitement of the event from a young child's perspective is *Carnival,* by ROBIN BALLARD (1995).

Return to Grand Army Plaza and, crossing Flatbush Avenue, take the 41 bus to the Lincoln Road stop (a short ride). Exiting the bus, walk along Lincoln for one block, cross Ocean Avenue, and enter **Prospect Park**. Bearing left along the footpath, continue on to the **Imagination Playground**. The centerpiece of this award-winning play and performance space is Otto Neals's sculpture of Peter, young hero of Ezra Jack Keats's *The Snowy Day* (1962), *Whistle for Willie* (1964), *Peter's Chair* (1967), and other Keats

Peter, by Otto Neals

picture books set in an impressionistically rendered version of the East New York, Brooklyn, of the author-artist's childhood. Neals's sculpture is designed for climbing and as a setting for storytelling. (Information: 718-965-8945; www.ezra-jack-keats.org)

More Brooklyn Books

The Alley, by ELEANOR ESTES, illustrated by EDWARD ARDIZZONE (1964). The enterprising children who live in the row of faculty housing at Pratt Institute (here re-named Grandby College) solve a burglary and mull over the meaning of life in typical deadpan Estes fashion. The author's husband was Pratt's library director for nearly twenty years. Visit the setting of this story by taking the G subway train to the Clinton and Washington stop and exiting on the Washington side. The "alley" can still be found behind the on-campus faculty housing on Emerson Place, Willoughby Avenue, and Steuben Street.

Brooklyn Doesn't Rhyme, by JOAN W. BLOS, illustrated by PAUL BIRLING (1994). Sixth-grader Rosey Sachs is a first-generation Polish-Jewish American living at

311 Hart Street, Bedford-Stuyvesant, at the turn of the last century. When her teacher encourages her to write from personal experience, Rosey discovers unsuspected meaning in her life at home.

Gowanus Dogs, by JONATHAN FROST (1999). In this picture book illustrated with powerful etchings, a homeless

Gowanus Dogs, *by Jonathan Frost*

man and a family of stray dogs make places for themselves in the bleak industrial cityscape along Brooklyn's Gowanus Canal.

In the Night Kitchen, by MAURICE SENDAK (1970). Set in a Winsor McCay–inspired comic-strip version of Brooklyn, this quintessential night-flight fantasy makes nostalgic reference to, among other local institutions, the aromatic Sunshine baking plant once located at the corner of Flatbush Avenue and Victory Boulevard and the elevated Brooklyn-Manhattan Transit (BMT) subway line that bore young Maurice to the Oz-like metropolis across the East River.

The Jetty Chronicles, by LEONARD EVERETT FISHER (1997). Memories of meetings with remarkable Brooklynites fill this informal memoir of growing up during the late 1930s in **Sea Gate**, the once exclusive gated coastal community west of Coney Island. Among the fascinating facts that young Leonard learns: The rocks used to form the jetty at Sea Gate (visible from the Coney Island boardwalk) are Manhattan schist, dynamited out of the ground during construction of the BMT subway line.

Last Summer with Maizon, by JACQUELINE WOODSON (1990). The strong friendship of two 11-year-olds living on Madison Street, in Bushwick, is put to the test when one of the girls, Margaret, loses her father and the other, Maizon, is offered a scholarship to a Connecticut private school.

Life Is Funny, by E.R. FRANK (2000), lets us listen in as eleven Brooklyn teens speak their minds about growing up in a world where teen pregnancy, domestic violence, and alcoholism are as commonplace as falling head-over-heels in love.

The Sign on Rosie's Door, by MAURICE SENDAK (1960). This freewheeling chapter book recalls a happy stretch in the author's youth when a group of neighborhood kids had a grand time making street theater out of their own young lives. The Sendaks, who moved frequently within Bensonhurst, were living just then in an apartment near the intersection of 69th Street (Bay Ridge Avenue) and 18th Avenue.

A Tree Grows in Brooklyn, by BETTY SMITH (1943). Set during the early 1900s in the hard-bitten Williamsburg section of Brooklyn, Smith's full-hearted coming-of-age saga traces the Nolan family's struggles to make ends meet while preserving their dignity.

When Pirates Came to Brooklyn, by PHYLLIS SHALANT (2002). Set in the ethnically mixed Flatlands section of Brooklyn in 1960, this novel tells the nuanced tale of a group of sixth-graders for whom coming to grips with their own and others' prejudices becomes intimately entwined with the games they play.

THE BRONX

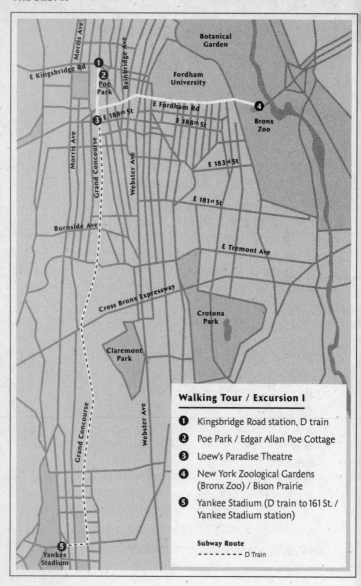

Walking Tour / Excursion I

❶ Kingsbridge Road station, D train

❷ Poe Park / Edgar Allan Poe Cottage

❸ Loew's Paradise Theatre

❹ New York Zoological Gardens
(Bronx Zoo) / Bison Prairie

❺ Yankee Stadium (D train to 161 St. /
Yankee Stadium station)

Subway Route

------- D Train

Walking Tour / Excursion II

Pelham Bay Park's Kazimiroff Trail

DIRECTIONS: Pelham Bay Park is located in the northeast corner of the Bronx.
Summer tours of Kazimiroff Trail leave from the Orchard Beach Nature Center.
To reach Pelham Bay Park, take the # 6 subway train to the Pelham Bay Park station.
From the subway, take the Bx 12 bus to Orchard Beach. The Bx 5 bus also runs
there on summer weekends. Be sure to call ahead to confirm tour times.
For information: 1-866-NYC-HAWK

Queens map is on page 125.
Staten Island map is on page 130.

THE BRONX

·

QUEENS

·

STATEN ISLAND

The Bronx

The only borough of New York City situated on the North American mainland (all the others are on islands), the Bronx derives its name from the area's first European settler, Jonas Bronck, who in 1639 established a farm on 500 acres north of the Harlem River. Today this northern-most borough of more than 1.2 million residents occupies 42 square miles.

Like northern Manhattan, Brooklyn, and Queens, the Bronx remained rural until the early nineteenth century, when rail service, the growth of industry, the arrival of European immigrant workers, and the availability of open land combined to make it ripe for development. Irish and Germans were the first Europeans to immigrate there in large numbers. By the late 1800s, the Bronx was also home to such important cultural institutions as the world-renowned New York Botanical Garden and Bronx Zoo, and to a broad, tree-lined boulevard, the Grand Concourse, intended to rival Paris's Champs-Élysées.

Italians, Jews, Yugoslavians, and Armenians were among the next groups to settle in the borough. In 1923 the New York Yankees, who until then had been sharing a ballpark in northern Manhattan with the Giants, opened Yankee Stadium at 161st Street and River Avenue, creating a new focus of pride for Bronx residents. After World War II, major population shifts occurred. Many longtime

Bronx residents moved to the suburbs. The south Bronx became a refuge for tens of thousands of poor and low-income Manhattanites who were being displaced by ill-conceived attempts at "urban renewal." By the 1970s, as property values declined, portions of the south Bronx had been reduced to rubble through arson and landlord neglect. Since that time, efforts to revitalize the area, and the borough as a whole, have met with some success.

WALKING TOUR / EXCURSION I

Our starting point is the Kingsbridge Road station of the D subway. Exiting the station, cross the street to nearby **Poe Park** and the **Edgar Allan Poe Cottage** (open for

guided tours Wed.–Fri. by appointment; Sat. 10 A.M.–4 P.M. and Sun. 1 P.M.–5 P.M.; 718-881-8900). The author of "The Raven" and "The Tell-Tale Heart" lived here from 1846 to 1849.

Although Poe never wrote expressly for children, his haunting lyrical poem "The Ballad of Ann-

Edgar Allan Poe Cottage

abel Lee," which he wrote while living here, is often anthologized for young readers and has been made into a picture book, *Annabel Lee: The Poem* (1987) by illustrator GILLES TIBO. An excellent young people's introduction to Poe's phantasmagoric short fiction is *Tales of Edgar Allan Poe*, illustrated by BARRY MOSER (1991).

References to Poe Cottage and its one-time resident help set the mock sinister tone of JILL PINKWATER's serio-comic *Tails of the Bronx* (1991), a novel that takes place on and around fictitious Burnbridge Avenue between 112th Street and 112th Avenue (said to be near the Grand Concourse; there *is* a Bainbridge Avenue just east of the cottage and a Burnside Avenue to the south).

"You've been reading too many of Mr. Poe's horrible stories," said Rochelle, who had returned as soon as the witch had walked away.

"They're not horrible," said The Raven. "They're works of art. The man was a Bronx genius."

"The man was a Bronx sick-o," said Rochelle.

The Raven backed his wheelchair over Rochelle's foot.

"Ouch!" she screamed, hopping around.

"Sorry," said The Raven, grinning.

"Don't mess with my man's main man," said Calvin, defending Edgar Allan Poe.

"Ever read one of his horror stories—if you can read, shrimp?" said Rochelle.

"Don't pick on my brother." I was ready to fight.

—Tails of the Bronx

Pinkwater depicts the Bronx in transition. Rochelle's ostentatiously upscale family insists on calling their refurbished row house a "brownstone." Yet a short walk from the block these children share are vast expanses of burned-out tenements, a grim no-man's-land that figures in the later, more serious chapters of Pinkwater's emotionally gritty, yet exuberant novel.

Walk south for two blocks on the Grand Concourse to East Fordham Road. Few signs remain along this stretch of the Concourse of its glory days during the 1930s and 1940s. Walk one block farther, however, to the corner of East 188th Street, to glimpse the majestic ghost of one of New York's great movie palaces, the long-shuttered Loew's Paradise. As you do so, think of a passage in JOHANNA HURWITZ's autobiographical novel, *Once I Was a Plum Tree* (1980). Hurwitz grew up to the southeast of this neighborhood during the late 1930s and 1940s, in a small apartment at 289 Bonner Place, in the unfashionable Melrose section of the Bronx.

Loew's Paradise Theatre, Grand Concourse

I once read in a book about people living on the wrong side of the tracks. There were some old, unused trolley tracks set in the cobblestones on Morris Avenue. My street was on one side of those tracks, and the kids on the Grand Concourse lived on

the other. . . . I supposed that Sheila and Marsha and Lois
were friends because they lived near each other.

—Once I Was a Plum Tree

Returning to East Fordham Road, take the Number 12 bus for the ten-minute ride to the main entrance of the **New York Zoological Gardens**, better known as the Bronx Zoo. You will want to spend hours here. Be sure to stop at the **Bison Prairie**, a three-acre expanse meant to evoke the bison's, or American buffalo's, natural habitat in the western United States. The Bison Prairie is located just beyond and to the left of the Italian-style fountain that you will see on entering via the zoo's gloriously ornamented bronze Rainey Gate.

As a child, Bronx-born picture-book artist NEIL WALDMAN came here often with his grandfather. Waldman recalls hearing the bison on view referred to, mysteriously, as "the Mother Herd." Years later, he and a librarian who was also curious about the meaning behind the phrase researched the question and discovered that at the turn of the last century, when the West's bison herds were nearing extinction, a group called the American Bison Society formed in the Bronx. The Society's aim was to restock the American prairie in part by breeding a buffalo herd at the zoo for reintroduction into the West. In ***They Came from the Bronx: How the Buffalo Were Saved from Extinction*** (2001), Waldman tells the im-

They Came from the Bronx: How the Buffalo Were Saved from Extinction, *by Neil Waldman*

probable and somehow very New York story of their spectacular success. For more true tales of this remarkable Bronx institution's past and present-day activities, read ***A Pelican Swallowed My Head***, by EDWARD R. RICCIUTI (2002).

If it is baseball season, you may want to return to Fordham Road and the Grand Concourse. Take the D train south to 161st Street/Yankee Stadium. **Yankee Stadium** is still often called "The House That Ruth Built" because it was Babe Ruth's crowd-thrilling, ticket-selling heroics that enabled the team's owners to finance the three-tiered extravaganza's construction in 1923. Two picture books recall the first golden age in the Yankees' ongoing saga. *Home Run*, by ROBERT BURLEIGH, illustrated by MIKE WIMMER (1998), portrays Babe

Home Run, *by Robert Burleigh, illustrated by Mike Wimmer*

Ruth in adoring, larger-than-life terms, while also providing a big enough ration of baseball statistics to satisfy most young fans. *Lou Gehrig: The Luckiest Man*, by DAVID A. ADLER, illustrated by TERRY WIDENER (1997), recounts the life of the great Yankee first baseman, who between 1925 and 1939 played in an amazing 2,130 consecutive games.

WALKING TOUR / EXCURSION II
The Kazimiroff Trail

Ever since my father originally told me the basic events in the life of Joe Two Trees, I have always felt this story was too valuable to lose.   —*The Last Algonquin*

Thus begins THEODORE KAZIMIROFF's *The Last Algonquin* (1982), a dramatic account of what must surely have been one of the more unusual friendships forged in New York City during the last century.

The author's father, Theodore, Sr., was a dentist by profession and a passionate amateur researcher who from childhood onward acquired a deep knowledge of Bronx history, archaeology, and nature lore. In 1924, as a Boy Scout hiking the wooded hills of Hunter and Twin Islands, in the northeast corner of the Bronx, he entered into the friendship of a lifetime. The man he met that day was Joe Two Trees, an aging member of the Turtle Clan of the Algonquin people, who after bitter experiences of discrimination in the white world of New York City had chosen to live in seclusion in the remote wild spaces of Pelham Bay Park. Knowing he did not have long to live, Joe Two Trees, who believed himself to be the last surviving member of his clan, entrusted the details of his personal history to the boy, who in turn relayed them to his son. *The Last Algonquin* is the son's record of that oral legacy.

During his last several months, Joe introduces Theodore to many aspects of craftsmanship and custom, as well as to a different perspective on time.

> *He opened the pouch. . . . First came a portion of a deer antler with two small tines protruding from it. I could tell that it was some sort of tool. . . . Joe said it was used in flaking the final point and edges on stone tools such as arrowheads . . .*
>
> *I was amazed to think that the deer that had once worn the antler had walked the woods of this very island. I was even more engrossed by the evident fact that the deer had been killed by Two Tree's great-grandfather, probably with an arrow tip of his own making. I began to feel very new to this world around me.* —The Last Algonquin

The elder Kazimiroff went on to unearth a vast trove of Native American artifacts, to advise both the Bronx Zoo and the New York Botanical Garden, and to found the Bronx Historical Society. Pelham Bay Park's Kazimiroff Trail is named for this devoted student of the Bronx.

The Kazimiroff Trail walking tour, which takes visitors to Hunter Island, is offered by the New York City Park Rangers on selected Sundays between Memorial Day and Labor Day, starting at 1 P.M. Tours leave from the Orchard Beach Nature Center, which can be reached via the Number 12 bus. For information: 1-866-NYC-HAWK.

More Bronx Books

All-of-a-Kind Family Uptown, by SYDNEY TAYLOR, illustrated by MARY STEVENS (1958). Having left the immigrant Lower East Side behind them, the five sisters and their parents have now moved up to the Bronx, and are living in an apartment within walking distance of Crotona Park.

Boy Without a Flag: Tales of the South Bronx, by ABRAHAM RODRIGUEZ (1992), is a collection of seven bracing stories about Puerto Rican teens desperate to feel at home in a city that offers them little they can call their own.

Bronx Masquerade, by NIKKI GRIMES (2002). While studying the Harlem Renaissance, students in a racially and ethnically diverse Bronx high school begin writing their own poetry, and discover for themselves—as they reveal to their classmates—the things that matter most in their lives.

The Diary of Latoya Hunter, by LATOYA HUNTER (1992). One year in the life and words of a Jamaican-born teen enrolled in the Isabel Rooney Middle School, in the Norwood section of the Bronx.

El Bronx Remembered, by NICHOLASA MOHR (1975). Eleven short stories and a novella, set during the years 1946–1956, evoke the raw and hard-edged tenement existence of Puerto Rican children growing up in the southeastern portion of the borough known as *El Bronx*.

The Gift-Giver, by JOYCE HANSEN (1980). In this tender but unsentimental coming-of-age story, fifth graders growing up in a neighborhood where random violence is a daily possibility learn to respect and watch out for one another. The action takes place on and around East 163rd Street in the Melrose section of the south Bronx.

Scooter, by VERA B. WILLIAMS (1993). The story of Elana Rose Rosen, a spunky girl who is good at making her own fun, and who more than holds her own as a child growing up in the projects of the north Bronx, near Mosholu Parkway and Van Cortlandt Park.

More Bronx Artists and Writers Over the Years

ASHLEY BRYAN • JULES FEIFFER • MAIRA KALMAN • ALBERT MARRIN • SEYMOUR SIMON • WILLIAM STEIG • SYDNEY TAYLOR

Queens

WALKING TOUR / EXCURSION

𝒯he largest New York City borough in land area, Queens, located on the northwestern tip of Long Island across the East River from Manhattan, may well be the most ethnically and racially diverse place in the world. Among its first inhabitants were members of the Maspeth family of the Rockaway tribe, who made their home on the present-day site of LaGuardia Airport. The Dutch arrived in the 1630s, followed soon afterward by the English, who first called the area Queens. Farming predominated until the 1830s, when the advent of rail service brought suburban, and later more densely packed urban development in its wake. Irish and Germans came in the first of many waves of immigrants from just about everywhere. Today, the public schools of one Queens neighborhood, Jackson Heights, serve children from seventy countries, speaking nearly forty different languages.

Our tour begins at the Number 7 line subway platform in Grand Central Terminal. Board the train on the Queens-bound side. There are at least two good reasons to do so. First, in 1999 the White House (in association

120 ▪ STORIED CITY

with the United States Department of Transportation and the Rails-to-Trails Conservancy) designated the Number 7, popularly known as the International Express, as a National Millenium Trail. The honor was bestowed in recognition of this train line's historic role as a vital conduit for the millions of immigrants who have made Queens their new home.

And second, the Number 7 line is itself the site of a series of striking artworks by Korean-American children's-book illustrator YUMI HEO. Heo had just completed work on a picture book, *A Is for Asia* (1997), when she devised an ambitious plan for a series of thirty colored-facet glass mosaic murals to be placed in three consecutive Number 7 line stations as part of the Metropolitan Transit Authority's Arts for Transit program. Installed on the mezzanine and platform levels of the **33rd Street/Rawson**, **40th Street/Lowery**, and **46th Street/Bliss** stations, the murals celebrate many aspects of Queens life and culture. From "A Is for Aqueduct Raceway" to "Z Is for Zoo" (featuring an image of the Queens Wildlife Center), Heo's luminous tableaux con-

Q Is for Queens *series,*
by Yumi Heo

stitute a unique picture book writ large across three of the borough's most heavily trafficked public spaces. They are well worth a visit.

Five stops farther into Queens from 46th Street/Bliss is the **82nd Street/Jackson Heights** station. While there are no book-related sites to see here, the area served by this station is itself the subject of an unusual picture-book history and guide. Illustrated by school-children, *Jackson Heights: From Ice Age to Space Age*, by RUDOLPH E. GRECO, JR., and CLAUDIA SOLOMON (1996), offers a delightful introduction to the growth and community life of this quiet, in some ways typical middle-class Queens residential neighborhood and its immediate surroundings. This locally published book, available in

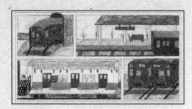

Jackson Heights: From Ice Age to Space Age, *by Rudolph E. Greco, Jr. and Claudia Solomon, illustrated by Queens schoolchildren*

Queens libraries, may well whet your appetite for a few hours of exploring on your own.

The artist who best captures the trimmed-hedge suburban side of Queens life is DAYAL KAUR KHALSA. Her picture books, based on memories of growing up during the 1950s in a section of the borough that might be Bellerose or Rosedale, include: *Tales of a Gambling Grandma* (1986), *How Pizza Came to Queens* (1989), and *Cowboy Dreams* (1990). Khalsa's wry, flamboyantly colored books also make a point of depicting Queens as a fine place to daydream. In the latter book, an

Cowboy Dreams, *by Dayal Kaur Khalsa*

imaginative young girl cherishes her Saturday afternoons spent at the movies, studying "how to be a cowboy, watching every move my cowboy heroes made." The movie palace where May receives her education in life on the prairie is the long-shuttered RKO Keith's Theater, located at the intersection of Northern Boulevard and Main Street, Flushing, five blocks north (along Main) from the last stop on the Number 7 train.

Continue on the Number 7 to the Willets Point/Shea Stadium station and follow the signs to the **Queens Museum of Art** (718-592-5555; www.queensmuse.org). This museum, located within Flushing Meadow-Corona Park, occupies the only building left over from both the 1939–40 and 1964–65 New York World's Fairs. The giant **Unisphere** (see Yumi Heo mural on page 121) in front of the museum served as the latter fair's focal point and symbol. While there is always some interesting special exhibit on view here, the museum's crowning glory is the **Panorama of the City of New York**—the world's largest scale model, representing in three dimensions, to a scale of one inch per one hundred feet, every extant building, bridge, street, railroad, and park in the entire city. In children's picture books about New York, far and away the most commonly expressed fantasy is that of a magical flight over a city, which, when viewed from ground level, can so easily overwhelm. To spend time gazing down at the Panorama from the elevated viewing platform is to experience a nearly comparable thrill.

During baseball season, you may of course want to combine your visit to the Queens Museum of Art with an

High Above New York in Picture Books

Abuela, by ARTHUR DORROS, illustrated by ELISA KLEVEN (1991). Rosalba, a New York Latino girl, and her *abuela*, or grandmother, share bird's-eye views of Queens, Manhattan, and New York harbor.

The Night Flight, by JOANNE RYDER, illustrated by AMY SCHWARTZ (1985). A brave girl dreams of flying over the city after dark.

Abuela, *by Arthur Dorros, illustrated by Elisa Kleven*

Wings, by CHRISTOPHER MYERS (2000). Ikarus Jackson, the new boy on the block, has magical wings and a mind of his own that, together, lift him above the ordinary.

afternoon or evening Mets game at nearby Shea Stadium. In *Baseball Fever*, illustrated by RAY CRUZ (1981), JO-HANNA HURWITZ writes about a 10-year-old Queens boy's intense love of the game and the conflict it leads to between him and his father, who can see no value in baseball.

More Queens Books

Fast Talk on a Slow Track, by RITA WILLIAMS-GARCIA (1991). Denzel Watson, an African-American honor student living in Jamaica, Queens, has one summer in which to choose between two very different possible futures, neither of which is clearly right for him.

Gina, by BERNARD WABER (1995). Gina is crestfallen on discovering there are no girls to play with in her new Kew Gardens Hills apartment building. Even so, the determined youngster makes many new friends.

Lily's Crossing, by PATRICIA REILLY GIFF (1997). " 'Rockaway.' *She said it aloud, loving the sound of it on her tongue. Rockaway and the ocean were waiting for her . . .*" This Newbery Honor novel recalls an all-but-vanished way of life—the seaside summer cottage communities of Rockaway, Queens. It is 1944, and 10-year-old Lily, who (like the author) comes from Irish-German St. Albans, runs the gamut of preteen emotions while also grappling with wartime fears and, yes, stopping to savor the sunsets.

Mama, Coming and Going,
by Judith Caseley

Mama, Coming and Going, by JUDITH CASELEY (1994). When Jenna's baby brother is born, Mama at first feels so overwhelmed that she is not always sure whether she is "coming or going." A series of comic mix-ups ensue, both at home (Bayside's Winsor Park Apartments, 211-06 75th Avenue, where the author once lived) and elsewhere around Queens.

Return to Manhattan via the Number 7 train, stopping to see the rest of Yumi Heo's radiant murals.

QUEENS

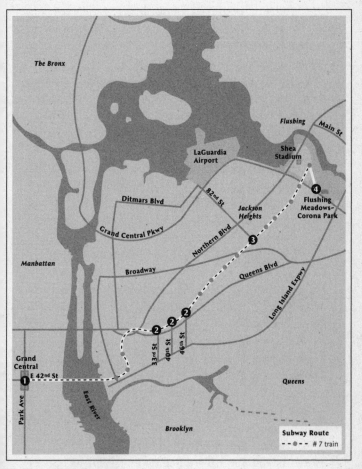

Walking Tour / Excursion

❶ Grand Central, #7 train

❷ 33rd St. / Rawson; 40th St. / Lowery; and 46th St. / Bliss stations (Yumi Heo murals)

❸ 82nd St. / Jackson Heights station

❹ Flushing Meadows–Corona Park Queens Museum of Art / Unisphere / (Willets Point / Shea Stadium station)

Staten Island

*T*he third largest and least populous of the city's five boroughs, Staten Island has a human prehistory that archaeologists have traced back 14,000 years. Raritan and Algonquin Indians lived here during the fifteenth and sixteenth centuries, followed first by Dutch and then British colonists. The island takes its name from the Netherlands' governing body, the States General or "Staten-general."

Until the completion of the Verrazano-Narrows Bridge in 1964, ferry service provided the only direct link between the island and the rest of New York. Partly for this reason, farming and fishing continued, longer than in other parts of the city, to dominate economic life. The island's strategic harbor location made it militarily important as well, and by the mid-nineteenth century Staten Island had also become a retreat for the rich and a manufacturing hub that attracted growing numbers of European immigrant workers. As industry declined during the Great Depression, the construction of numerous public-works projects helped buoy the local economy. In 1948, Fresh Kills Landfill opened as a repository for the city's trash. This controversial waste-disposal facility, which finally closed in 2001, grew to become the world's largest—even as Staten Island as a whole emerged as the city's most heavily residential borough.

WALKING TOUR / EXCURSION

This tour begins at the southern tip of Manhattan, at the **Staten Island Ferry Terminal** (foot of Whitehall Street at Battery Park; 718-815-2628).

Countless New Yorkers and tourists alike have taken the refreshing twenty-five-minute ferry ride, which departs from here at frequent intervals throughout the day, just for the fun of it. The Staten Island Ferry, which once cost a nickel, is now free; better still, riders may make as many crossings as they wish.

St. George Ferry Terminal,
Staten Island

A behind-the-scenes introduction to this centuries-old commuter service is provided in ***Riding the Ferry with Captain Cruz***, by ALICE K. FLANAGAN, photographed by CHRISTINE OSINSKI (1996). The author and photographer document a typical morning run of the *Andrew J. Barberi*, and explain the captain's role in helping people "get to work safely and on time."

A late-night ferry ride with a friend inspired the ever romantic Edna St. Vincent Millay to write "Recuerdo" (Spanish for "remembrance"), a lyric poem about the experience. In ***Edna*** (2000), illustrated by JOANNA YARDLEY, author ROBERT BURLEIGH offers an imaginative reconstruction of the crossing along with a biographical sketch of one of Greenwich Village's most ardently bohemian resident writers.

Far and away the writer for young people most closely associated with Staten Island is PAUL ZINDEL, who grew up in **Travis**, a modest west-shore neighborhood not far from the Fresh Kills Landfill. Known for his unflinchingly honest novels of teenage alienation and rebellion, Zindel has set many books on the island.

Zindel's now classic first young-adult novel, ***The Pigman*** (1968), takes place in Stapleton and Grymes Hill,

Edna, by Robert Burleigh, illustrated by Joanna Yardley

contiguous neighborhoods closer than Travis to the ferry landing. It's with characteristic candor that the author describes the home of Angelo Pignati (aka the Pigman), the older man at whose expense two high school sophomores play a random practical joke:

One-ninety Howard Avenue turned out to be just across the street from a big convent, and there were lots of trees and stuff and nuns running around the place. There were a lot of nice houses on the street too, but one-ninety was a phenomenal dump.
                                                                    —*The Pigman*

(Howard Avenue is a busy street in this part of Staten Island, but there is no house at that address.)

The threesome visit the **Staten Island Zoo** (614 Broadway; 718-442-3100; www.statenislandzoo.org). This small zoo, which is best known for its **Carl F. Kauffeld Hall of Reptiles,** may be reached by taking the S48 bus from the ferry terminal to the Forest Avenue and Broadway stop. Turning left onto Broadway, walk three blocks to the zoo entrance.

The zoo serves as a sardonic backdrop for the personalities of each of the novel's three lost souls: the lonely

Staten Island Zoo

Pigman, whose affection for the resident baboon seems painfully sad; John, whose fascination with the raptors mirrors his own capacity for cruelty; and Lorraine, whose need to remain above it all masks her emotional insecurity.

In his memoir for teen readers, *The Pigman & Me* (1991), Zindel recalls his first impressions of Travis, where he and his family lived starting in the 1940s.

When we first drove into the town, I noticed a lot of plain wood houses, a Catholic church, a war memorial, three saloons with men sitting outside on chairs, seventeen women wearing kerchiefs on their heads, a one-engine firehouse, a big red-brick school, a candy store, and a butcher shop with

about 300 sausages hanging in the window. . . . Travis was
mainly a Polish town, and was so special-looking that, years
later, it was picked as a location for filming the movie
Splendor in the Grass. *. . . Travis was selected because they*
needed a town that looked like it was Kansas in 1920, which
it still looks like. —The Pigman & Me

Zindel lived with his older sister and their mother in a
modest two-story house that once stood at 123 Glen
Street, by the intersection with Victory Boulevard.
Across the street was a now-abandoned cemetery, with a
run-down, long-gone airport in the distance beyond the
backyard. The house was demolished in the early 1960s
to make way for a service road for the new West Shore
Expressway, the construction of which completely transformed Travis. The area's place-that-time-forgot am-
biance was largely lost. Little besides the volunteer
Oceanic Hook & Ladder Company (4010 Victory Blvd.,
corner of Burke), six blocks north of Glen, remains of the
old-fashioned neighborhood of the author's youth (not
that Zindel has ever been overly nostalgic for the scenes
of his early unhappiness).

Undoubtedly the best day of the year for fans to make
the pilgrimage is on July 4, when, by an odd coincidence,
Travis's still-rousing, traditional Independence Day pa-
rade steps off from more or less the exact site of the old
Zindel homestead, at the intersection of Victory and
Glen. Travis can be reached by taking the S62 bus from
the ferry terminal to the corner of Victory Boulevard and
Burke Avenue.

Another of Zindel's Staten Island books, **Rats** (1999),
belongs to the contemporary genre of the eco-horror
story. In this blood-and-guts fantasy set in and around
the **Fresh Kills Landfill**, which is located just west of
Travis, the author imagines plaguelike swarms of rats ris-
ing up out of the landfill's murky depths to overrun portions of Staten Island and Manhattan, brutally attacking
everyone in their path. Given the hubris of those respon-
sible for Staten Island's mountains of trash (the tallest
peak at Fresh Kills is in fact the highest point on the east-

ern seaboard), it is hard not to react with mixed emotion to the sorry fates of the city personnel who fall prey to the ravenous rodents. In Zindel's fiction, in any case, there are never clear winners, only survivors who come to know themselves and their fellows a bit better, or fail to do so at their peril.

STATEN ISLAND

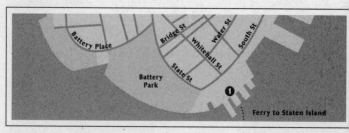

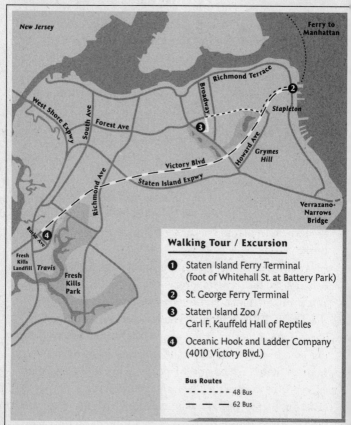

Walking Tour / Excursion

❶ Staten Island Ferry Terminal
(foot of Whitehall St. at Battery Park)

❷ St. George Ferry Terminal

❸ Staten Island Zoo /
Carl F. Kauffeld Hall of Reptiles

❹ Oceanic Hook and Ladder Company
(4010 Victory Blvd.)

Bus Routes
- - - - - - - - 48 Bus
— — — — 62 Bus

Ten More Ways to See New York

Alphabetically ▪ *Alphabet City*, by STEPHEN T. JOHNSON (1995). Photo-realist paintings present a complete set of letter-forms that the artist observed while roaming the city.

Architecturally ▪ *The Inside-Outside Book of New York City*, by ROXIE MUNRO (1985, 2001). An artist with a knack for capturing the essence of a place surveys a variety of the city's famous attractions.

As a cat ▪ *Black Cat*, by CHRISTOPHER MYERS (1999). A cat finds that wandering New York's streets (and rooftops) is a good way to learn about the city and himself.

As a gorilla ▪ *The Escape of Marvin the Ape*, by CARALYN and MARK BUEHNER (1992). New Yorkers' legendary been-there-done-that view of life gets stretched to the limit in this tale about a great ape on the lam from the zoo.

Botanically ▪ *Wild Green Things in the City: A Book of Weeds*, by ANNE OPHELIA DOWDEN (1972). A botanical artist's field guide to the leafy and flowering things that grow unbidden all around town.

By cab ▪ *The Adventures of Taxi Dog*, by DEBRA and SAL BARRACCA; illustrated by MARK BUEHNER (1990). Maxi the dog teams up with a New York taxi driver to entertain any and all comers who land in the backseat of the cab.

Historically ▪ *A Short and Remarkable History of New York City*, by JANE MUSHABAC and ANGELA WIGAN; illustrated with art from the Museum of the City of New York (1999). An anecdote-rich timeline, from prehistory through the year 1998.

Numerically ▪ *City by Numbers*, STEPHEN T. JOHNSON (1998). The creator of *Alphabet City* goes hunting again, this time for number-forms, from 0 to 21.

Ornithologically ▪ *Urban Roosts: Where Birds Nest in the City*, by BARBARA BASH (1990). Where to look for birds in the contemporary skyscraper city.

Poetically ▪ *Sky Scrape/City Scape*, selected by JANE YOLEN; illustrated by KEN CONDON (1996). Poems about New York life by Eve Merriam, Langston Hughes, Lucille Clifton, Lee Bennett Hopkins, and others.

Bibliography

■

Boldface numbers in brackets indicate age level of book.
{1} ages 4–8   {2} ages 8–12   {3} ages 12 and up

Adler, David A. *Lou Gehrig: The Luckiest Man*. Illustrated by Terry Widener. San Diego: Harcourt, 1997. {1}

Alger, Horatio, Jr. *Ragged Dick or, Street Life in New York with the Boot-Blacks*. Boston: Loring, 1867. {3}

Ancona, George. *Cutters, Carvers & the Cathedral*. New York: Lothrop, 1995. {2}

Anglund, Joan Walsh. *Love Is a Special Way of Feeling*. New York: Harcourt Brace, 1960. {1}

Anonymous. *'Twas the Night Before Christmas or Account of a Visit from St. Nicholas*. Illustrated by Matt Tavares. Cambridge, MA: Candlewick, 2002. {1}

Auch, Mary Jane. *Ashes of Roses*. New York: Holt, 2002. {3}

Averill, Esther. *Jenny and the Cat Club*. New York: New York Review of Books, 2003. {1}

Ballard, Robin. *Carnival*. New York: Greenwillow, 1995. {1}

Barracca, Debra and Sal. *The Adventures of Taxi Dog*. Illustrated by Mark Buehner. New York: Dial, 1990. {1}

Bartoletti, Susan Campbell. *Black Potatoes: The Story of the Great Irish Potato Famine, 1845–1850*. Boston: Houghton Mifflin, 2002. {3}

Bartone, Elisa. *Peppe the Lamplighter*. Illustrated by Ted Lewin. New York: Lothrop, 1993. {1}

Bash, Barbara. *Urban Roosts: Where Birds Nest in the City*. Boston: Little, Brown, 1990. {1}

Bausum, Ann. *Dragon Bones and Dinosaur Eggs: A Photobiography of Explorer Roy Chapman Andrews*. Washington, D.C.: National Geographic Society, 2000. {2}

Bearden, Romare, illustrator. *The Block*. Poems by Langston Hughes. New York: The Metropolitan Museum of Art/Viking, 1995. {2}

Bemelmans, Ludwig. *Madeline*. New York: Simon and Schuster, 1939. [1]

Bial, Raymond. *Tenement: Immigrant Life on the Lower East Side*. Boston: Houghton Mifflin, 2002. {3}

Bjork, Christina, and Inga-Karin Eriksson. *The Other Alice: The Story of Alice Liddell and* Alice in Wonderland. Stockholm and New York: R and S, 1993. {2}

Blos, Joan W. *Brooklyn Doesn't Rhyme*. Illustrated by Paul Birling. New York: Scribner, 1994. {2}

Blume, Judy. *Double Fudge*. New York: Dutton, 2002. {2}

———. *Superfudge*. New York: Dutton, 1980. {2}

———. *Tales of a Fourth Grade Nothing*. Illustrated by Roy Doty. New York: Dutton, 1972. {2}

Brooks, Walter R. *To and Again* (reissued as *Freddy Goes to Florida*). Freddy the Pig series. New York: A.A. Knopf, 1927. {2}

Brown, Marcia. *Cinderella; or, The Little Glass Slipper*. New York: Scribner, 1954. {1}

Brown, Margaret Wise. *Goodnight Moon*. Pictures by Clement Hurd. New York: Harper, 1947. {PreS}

———. *Mister Dog, or The Dog Who Belonged to Himself.* Illustrated by Garth Williams. New York: Simon and Schuster, 1952. {1}

———. *The Runaway Bunny*. Pictures by Clement Hurd. New York: Harper, 1942. {PreS}

Brust, Beth Wagner. *The Amazing Paper Cuttings of Hans Christian Andersen*. New York: Ticknor & Fields, 1994. {2}

Buehner, Caralyn and Mark. *The Escape of Marvin the Ape*. New York: Dial, 1992. {1}

Burleigh, Robert. *Edna*. Illustrated by Joanna Yardley. New York: Orchard, 2000. {1}

———. *Home Run: The Story of Babe Ruth*. Illustrated by Mike Wimmer. San Diego: Harcourt, 1998. {1}

Burnett, Frances Hodgson. *Little Lord Fauntleroy*. New York: Scribners, 1886. {2}

———. *A Little Princess*. New York: Scribners, 1905. {2}

———. *The Secret Garden*. New York: Grosset & Dunlap, 1911. {2}

Byrd, Donald. *The Harlem Nutcracker*. Photographed by Susan Kuklin. New York: Hyperion, 2001. {2}

Cart, Michael, et al. (eds.) *911—The Book of Help*. Chicago: Cricket, 2002. {3}

Caseley, Judith. *Mama, Coming and Going*. New York: Greenwillow, 1994. {1}

Cohen, Miriam. *Eddy's Dream*. Photographed by Adam Cohen. New York: Star Bright, 2000. {1}

Collier, Bryan. *Uptown*. New York: Holt, 2000. {1}

Collier, James Lincoln. *The Teddy Bear Habit*. Illustrated by Lee Lorenz. New York: Grosset & Dunlap, 1967. {2}

———, and Christopher Collier. *War Comes to Willy Freeman*. New York: Delacorte, 1983. {2}

———. *Who Is Carrie?*. New York: Delacorte, 1984. {2}

Cooney, Barbara. *Hattie and the Wild Waves*. New York: Viking, 1990. {1}

Corey, Shana. *Milly and the Macy's Parade*. Illustrated by Brett Helquist. New York: Scholastic, 2002. {1}

Costabel, Eva Deutsch. *The Jews of New Amsterdam*. New York: Atheneum, 1988. {1}

Crews, Donald. *Harbor*. New York: Greenwillow, 1982. {1}

Curlee, Lynn. *Brooklyn Bridge*. New York: Atheneum, 2001. {2}

———. *Liberty*. New York: Atheneum, 2000. {2}

Dahl, Roald. *James and the Giant Peach*. Illustrated by Nancy Ekholm Burkert. New York: Knopf, 1961; re-illustrated by Quentin Blake, 1995. {2}

Daigon, Ruth. *Payday at the Triangle*. Concord: Small Poetry Press (P.O. Box 5342, Concord, CA 94524), 2001. {3}

Danziger, Paula. *Remember Me to Harold Square*. New York: Delacorte, 1987. {2}

Daugherty, James. *Andy and the Lion: A Tale of Kindness Remembered or the Power of Gratitude*. New York: Viking, 1938. {1}

D'Aulaire, Ingri, and Edgar Parin d'Aulaire. *D'Aulaires' Book of Greek Myths*. New York: Doubleday, 1962. {1}

Davies, Valentine. *Miracle on 34th Street*. New York: Harcourt, 1947. {2}

Day, Mahlon. *New York Street Cries in Rhyme*. New York: Day, 1825; Edited by Leonard S. Marcus (New York: Dover, 1977). {1}

Demi. *Gandhi*. New York: Margaret K. McElderry, 2001. {1}

Dingle, Derek T. *First in the Field: Baseball Hero Jackie Robinson*. New York: Hyperion, 1998. {2}

Dorros, Arthur. *Abuela*. Illustrated by Elisa Kleven. New York: Dutton, 1991. {1}

Dowden, Anne Ophelia. *Wild Green Things in the City: A Book of Weeds*. New York: Crowell, 1972. {2}

Drummond, Allan. *Liberty!*. New York: Frances Foster/Farrar, Straus & Giroux, 2002. {1}

Duane, Diane. *So You Want to Be a Wizard*. New York: Delacorte, 1983. {3}

Duggleby, John. *Story Painter: The Life of Jacob Lawrence*. San Francisco: Chronicle, 1998. {2}

Egielski, Richard. *The Gingerbread Boy*. New York: Laura Geringer/Harper, 1997. {1}

Emerson, Caroline D. *The Magic Tunnel*. Illustrated by Raymond Lufkin. New York: Stokes, 1940. Re-illustrated by Jerry Robinson. New York: Four Winds, 1964. {2}

Enright, Elizabeth. *The Saturdays*. New York: Holt, 1941. {2}

Estes, Eleanor. *The Alley*. Illustrated by Edward Ardizzone. New York: Harcourt, 1964. {2}

————. *Ginger Pye*. New York: Harcourt, 1951. {2}

Field, Rachel. *All This, and Heaven Too*. New York: The Macmillan Company, 1938.

Fisher, Leonard Everett. *The Jetty Chronicles*. Tarrytown: Marshall Cavendish, 1997. {2}

Fitzhugh, Louise. *Harriet the Spy*. New York: Harper, 1964. {2}

Flanagan, Alice K. *Riding the Ferry with Captain Cruz*. Photographed by Christine Osinski. Danbury, CT: Children's Press, 1996. {1}

Frank, E.R. *Life Is Funny*. New York: DK, 2000. {3}

Frank, Mitch. *Understanding September 11th: Answering Questions About the Attacks on America*. New York: Viking, 2002. {3}

Freeman, Don, and Lydia Freeman. *Pet of the Met*. New York: Viking, 1953. {1}

Freedman, Russell. *Immigrant Kids*. New York: Dutton, 1980. {2}

————. *Lincoln: A Photobiography*. New York: Clarion, 1987. {2}

Fritz, Jean. *Bully for You, Teddy Roosevelt!*. Illustrated by Mike Wimmer. New York: Putnam, 1991. {2}

————. *Why Not, Lafayette?*. Illustrated by Ronald Himler. New York: Putnam, 1999. {2}

Frost, Jonathan. *Gowanus Dogs*. New York: Frances Foster/Farrar, Straus & Giroux, 1999. {1}

Ganci, Chris. *Chief: The Life of Peter J. Ganci*. New York: Orchard, 2003. {2}

Giff, Patricia Reilly. *Lily's Crossing*. New York: Delacorte, 1997. {2}

Giovanni, Nikki. *Shimmy Shimmy Shimmy Like My Sister Kate: Looking at the Harlem Renaissance Through Poems*. New York: Holt, 1996. {3}

Golenbock, Peter. *Teammates*. Illustrated by Paul Bacon. San Diego: Harcourt, 1990. {1}

Gramatky, Hardie. *Little Toot*. New York: Putnam, 1939. {1}

Granfield, Linda. *97 Orchard Street, New York*. Photographed by Arlene Alda. Montreal: Tundra, 2001. {2}

Gray, Luli. *Falcon's Egg*. Boston: Houghton Mifflin, 1995. {2}

Greco, Rudolph E., Jr., and Claudia Solomon. *Jackson Heights from Ice Age to Space Age: A History for Children*. Illustrated by the children of Jackson Heights. New York: Jackson Heights Beautification Group (P.O. Box 253, Jackson Heights, NY 11372), 1996. {2}

Griffin, Adele. *The Other Shepards*. New York: Hyperion, 1998. {2}

Grimes, Nikki. *Bronx Masquerade*. New York: Dial, 2002. {3}

Guy, Rosa. *Edith Jackson*. New York: Viking, 1978. {3}

———. *The Friends*. New York: Holt, 1973. {3}

———. *Ruby*. New York: Viking, 1976. {3}

Hamilton, Virginia. *The Planet of Junior Brown*. New York: Macmillan, 1971. {2}

Hansen, Joyce. *The Gift-Giver*. New York: Clarion, 1980. {2}

———, and Gary McGowan. *Breaking Ground, Breaking Silence: The Story of New York's African Burial Ground*. New York: Holt, 1998. {2}

Hartfield, Claire. *Me and Uncle Romie*. Illustrated by Jerome Lagarrigue. New York: Dial, 2002. {1}

Haskins, Jim. *The Harlem Renaissance*. Brookfield, CT: Millbrook, 1996. {2}

Havens, Catherine E. *Diary of a Little Girl in Old New York*. Bedford, MA: Applewood, 2001. {2}

Henry, O. *The Gift of the Magi and Other Stories*. Illustrated by Michael Dooling. New York: Books of Wonder/Morrow, 1997. {3}

Heo, Yumi. *One Summer Morning*. New York: Orchard, 1999. {1}

Hesse, Karen. *Letters from Rifka*. New York: Holt, 1992. {2}

High, Linda Oatman. *Under New York*. Illustrated by Robert Rayevsky. New York: Holiday House, 2001. {1}

Hine, Lewis W. *Men at Work*. New York: Macmillan, 1932. {2}

Holman, Felice. *Slake's Limbo*. New York: Atheneum, 1974. {3}

Hughes, Langston. *Black Misery*. Illustrated by Arouni. New York: Eriksson, 1969. {2}

———. *The Dream Keeper and Other Poems*. Illustrated by Helen Sewell. New York: Knopf, 1932; re-illustrated by Brian Pinkney, 1994. {1}

———. *The Sweet and Sour Animal Book*. Illustrated by students of the Harlem School of the Arts. New York: Oxford, 1994. {1}

Hunter, Latoya. *The Diary of Latoya Hunter: My First Year in Junior High*. New York: Crown, 1992. {3}

Hurwitz, Johanna. *Baseball Fever*. Illustrated by Ray Cruz. New York: Morrow, 1981. {2}

———. *Busybody Nora*. Illustrated by Susan Jeschke. New York: Morrow, 1976; re-illustrated by Lillian Hoban, 1990. {2}

———. *Once I Was a Plum Tree*. Illustrated by Ingrid Fetz. New York: Morrow, 1980. {2}

Irving, Washington. *The Legend of Sleepy Hollow*. Illustrated by Will Moses. New York: Philomel, 1995. {1}

———. *Rip Van Winkle*. Illustrated by Will Moses. New York: Philomel, 1999. {1}

Jakobsen, Kathy. *My New York*. Boston: Little, Brown, 1993. {1}

Jocelyn, Marthe. *The Invisible Day*. Illustrated by Abby Carter. New York: Dutton, 1997. {2}

Johnson, Stephen T. *Alphabet City*. New York: Viking, 1995. {1}

———. *City by Numbers*. New York: Viking, 1998. {1}

Kalman, Maira. *Fireboat: The Heroic Adventures of the* John J. Harvey. New York: Putnam, 2002. {1}

———. *Next Stop Grand Central*. New York: Putnam, 1999. {1}

Kamen, Gloria. *Fiorello: His Honor, the Little Flower*. New York: Atheneum, 1981. {2}

Katz, William Loren. *Black Legacy: A History of New York's African Americans*. New York: Atheneum, 1997. {2}

Kazimiroff, Theodore L. *The Last Algonquin*. New York: Walker, 1982. {3}

Keats, Ezra Jack. *Peter's Chair*. New York: Harper, 1967. {1}

———. *Skates*. New York: Watts, 1973. {1}

———. *The Snowy Day*. New York: Viking, 1962. {1}

———. *Whistle for Willie*. New York: Viking, 1964. {1}

Kerley, Barbara. *The Dinosaurs of Waterhouse Hawkins*. Illustrated by Brian Selznick. New York: Scholastic, 2001. {1}

Kerr, M.E. *Dinky Hocker Shoots Smack!* New York: Harper, 1972. {3}

Khalsa, Dayal Kaur. *Cowboy Dreams*. New York: Potter, 1990. {1}

———. *How Pizza Came to Queens*. New York: Potter, 1989. {1}

———. *Tales of a Gambling Grandma*. New York: Potter, 1986. {1}

Konigsburg, E.L. *From the Mixed-up Files of Mrs. Basil E. Frankweiler*. New York: Atheneum, 1967. {2}

Krizner, L.J., and Lisa Sita. *Peter Stuyvesant: New Amsterdam and the Origins of New York*. New York: Rosen/PowerPlus Books, 2002. {2}

Kroll, Steven. *Sweet America: An Immigrant's Story*. Chicago: Jamestown, 2000. {3}

Kuskin, Karla. *The Philharmonic Gets Dressed*. Illustrated by Marc Simont. New York: Charlotte Zolotow/Harper, 1982. {1}

Lasky, Kathryn. *Dreams of the Golden Country: The Diary of Ziporah Feldman, a Jewish Immigrant Girl, New York City, 1903*. New York: Scholastic, 1998. {2}

Lawler, Mary. *Marcus Garvey: Black Nationalist Leader*. New York and Philadelphia: Chelsea House, 1988. {3}

Lawlor, Veronica. *I Was Dreaming to Come to America: Memories from the Ellis Island Oral History Project*. New York: Viking, 1995. {1}

Lawrence, Jacob. *The Great Migration: An American Story*. New York: Museum of Modern Art/Harper, 1993. {1}

L'Engle, Madeleine. *Meet the Austins*. New York: Vanguard Press, 1960. {3}

———. *A Ring of Endless Light*. New York: Farrar, Straus and Giroux, 1980. {3}

———. *The Young Unicorns*. New York: Farrar, Straus & Giroux, 1968. {3}

Levine, Ellen. . . . *If Your Name Was Changed at Ellis Island*. Illustrated by Wayne Parmenter. New York: Scholastic, 1993. {2}

Levine, Gail Carson. *Dave at Night*. New York: Harper, 1999. {2}

Lipkind, Will. *The Two Reds*. Illustrated by Nicolas Mordvinoff. New York: Harcourt, 1950. {1}

Lipsyte, Robert. *The Contender*. New York: Harper, 1967. {1}

Littlefield, Holly. *Fire at the Triangle Factory*. Illustrated by Mary O'Keefe Young. Minneapolis: Carolrhoda, 1996. {3}

Lobel, Arnold. *On the Day Peter Stuyvesant Sailed into Town*. New York: Harper, 1971. {1}

Lord, Bette Bao. *In the Year of the Boar and Jackie Robinson*. Illustrated by Marc Simont. New York: HarperCollins, 1984. {2}

Low, William. *Chinatown*. New York: Holt, 1997. {1}

Lowry, Lois. *The Giver*. Boston: Houghton Mifflin, 1993. {3}

———. *Number the Stars*. Boston: Houghton Mifflin, 1989. {3}

Macaulay, David. *Unbuilding*. Boston: Houghton Mifflin, 1980. {2}

Maestro, Betsy, and Giulio Maestro. *The Story of the Statue of Liberty!* New York: Lothrop, 1986. {1}

Mak, Kam. *My Chinatown: One Year in Poems*. New York: Harper, 2001. {1}

Marrin, Albert. *George Washington & the Founding of a Nation*. New York: Dutton, 2001. {3}

———. *Secrets from the Rocks: Dinosaur Hunting with Roy Chapman Andrews*. New York: Dutton, 2002. {2}

McCay, Winsor. *Dreams of the Rarebit Fiend*. New York: Dover, 1973. {3}

McCloskey, Robert. *Make Way for Ducklings*. New York: Viking Press, 1941. {1}

Medina, Tony. *Love to Langston*. Illustrated by R. Gregory Christie. New York: Lee & Low, 2002. {1}

Merrill, Jean. *The Pushcart War*. Illustrated by Ronni Solbert. New York: HarperCollins, 1964. {2}

Minarik, Else Holmelund. *Little Bear*. Pictures by Maurice Sendak. New York: Harper, 1957. {1}

Mohr, Nicholasa. *El Bronx Remembered*. New York: Harper, 1975. {3}

———. *Felita*. New York: Dial, 1979. {2}

———. *Nilda*. New York: Harper, 1973. {3}

Moore, Clement C. *The Night Before Christmas*. Illustrated by Raquel Jaramillo. New York: Anne Schwartz/Atheneum, 2001. {1}

———. *The Night Before Christmas*. Illustrated by Bruce Whatley. New York: Harper, 1999. {1}

———. *The Night Before Christmas Coloring Book*. Illustrated by John O'Brien. New York: Dover, 1981. {1}

Munro, Roxie. *The Inside-Outside Book of New York City*. New York: Dodd, Mead, 1985; SeaStar, 2001. {1}

Mushabac, Jane, and Angela Wigan. *A Short and Remarkable History of New York City*. New York: Fordham University Press, 1999. {3}

Myers, Christopher. *Black Cat*. New York: Scholastic, 1999. {1}

———. *Wings*. New York: Scholastic, 2000. {1}

Myers, Walter Dean. *Bad Boy: A Memoir*. New York: Amistad/Harper, 2001. {3}

———. *Harlem*. Illustrated by Christopher Myers. New York: Scholastic, 1997. {1}

———. *Malcolm X: A Fire Burning Brightly*. Illustrated by Leonard Jenkins. New York: Harper, 2000. {1}

———. *Malcolm X: By Any Means Necessary*. New York: Scholastic, 1993. {3}

———. *Monster*. Illustrated by Christopher Myers. New York: Harper, 1999. {3}

———. *145th Street: Short Stories*. New York: Delacorte, 2000. {3}

———. *Scorpions*. New York: Harper, 1988. {3}

Neumann, Dietrich. *Joe and the Skyscraper*. New York: Prestel, 1999. {1}

Neville, Emily Cheney. *It's Like This, Cat*. Illustrated by Emil Weiss. New York: Harper, 1963. {2}

Nikola-Lisa, W. *Bein' with You This Way*. Illustrated by Michael Bryant. New York: Lee & Low, 1994. {1}

O'Hara, Mary. *My Friend Flicka*. Philadelphia: Lippincott, 1941. {2}

Osborne, Mary Pope. *New York's Bravest*. Illustrated by Steve Johnson and Lou Fancher. New York: Knopf, 2002. {1}

Perdomo, Willie. *Visiting Langston*. Illustrated by Bryan Collier. New York: Holt, 2002. {1}

Pinkney, Andrea Davis. *Alvin Ailey*. Illustrated by Brian Pinkney. New York: Hyperion, 1993. {1}

———. *Duke Ellington*. Illustrated by Brian Pinkney. New York: Hyperion, 1998. {1}

———. *Mim's Christmas Jam*. Illustrated by Brian Pinkney. San Diego: Harcourt, 2001. {1}

Pinkwater, Jill. *Tails of the Bronx*. New York: Macmillan, 1991. {2}

Poe, Edgar Allan. *Annabel Lee: The Poem*. Illustrated by Gilles Tibo. Montreal: Tundra, 1987. {1}

———. *Tales of Edgar Allan Poe*. Illustrated by Barry Moser. New York: Books of Wonder/Morrow, 1991. {3}

Rael, Elsa Okon. *What Zeesie Saw on Delancey Street*. Illustrated by Marjorie Priceman. New York: Simon and Schuster, 1996. {1}

———. *When Zaydeh Danced on Eldridge Street*. Illustrated by Marjorie Priceman. New York: Simon and Schuster, 1997. {1}

Rawlings, Marjorie Kinnan. *The Yearling*. New York: Scribners, 1938. {3}

Rey, H.A. *Curious George*. Boston: Houghton Mifflin, 1941. {1}

———. *Find the Constellations*. Boston: Houghton Mifflin, 1954. {2}

Ricciuti, Edward R. *A Pelican Swallowed My Head, and Other Zoo Stories from the Wildlife Conservation Society*. New York: Simon and Schuster, 2002. {2}

Richardson, Joy. *Inside the Museum: A Children's Guide to the Metropolitan Museum of Art*. New York: Abrams, 1993. {2}

Ringgold, Faith. *Tar Beach*. New York: Crown, 1991. {1}

Rodgers, Mary. *Freaky Friday*. New York: Harper, 1972. {2}

Rodriguez, Abraham. *Boy Without a Flag: Tales of the South Bronx*. Minneapolis, MN: Milkweed, 1992. {3}

Roehrig, Catharine. *Fun with Hieroglyphs*. The Metropolitan Museum of Art/Viking, 1990. {2}

Roth, Susan L. *Happy Birthday Mr. Kang*. Washington, D.C.: National Geographic Society, 2001. {1}

Rush, Ken. *Friday's Journey*. New York: Orchard, 1994. {1}

Ryder, Joanne. *The Night Flight*. Illustrated by Amy Schwartz. New York: Four Winds, 1985. {1}

Salinger, J.D. *The Catcher in the Rye*. Boston: Little, Brown, 1951. {3}

Sawyer, Ruth. *Roller Skates*. Illustrated by Valenti Angelo. New York: Viking, 1936. {2}

Schwartz, Amy. *A Teeny Tiny Baby*. New York: Orchard, 1994. {1}

Scieszka, Jon. *2095*. Illustrated by Lane Smith. New York: Viking, 1995. {2}

Seidler, Tor. *A Rat's Tale*. Illustrated by Fred Marcellino. New York: Farrar, Straus & Giroux, 1986. {2}

Selden, George. *Chester Cricket's Pigeon Ride.* Illustrated by Garth Williams. New York: Farrar, Straus & Giroux, 1981. {2}

———. *The Cricket in Times Square.* Illustrated by Garth Williams. New York: Farrar, Straus & Giroux, 1960. {2}

Sendak, Maurice. *In the Night Kitchen.* New York: Harper, 1970. {1}

———. *The Sign on Rosie's Door.* New York: Harper, 1960. {1}

———. *Where the Wild Things Are.* New York: Harper, 1963. {1}

Severance, John B. *Gandhi: Great Soul.* New York: Clarion, 1997. {3}

Shalant, Phyllis. *When Pirates Came to Brooklyn.* New York: Dutton, 2002. {2}

Simon, Seymour. *The Universe.* New York: Morrow, 1998. {1}

Sís, Peter. *Follow the Dream: The Story of Christopher Columbus.* New York: Knopf, 1991. {1}

———. *Madlenka.* New York: Frances Foster/Farrar, Straus & Giroux, 2000. {1}

Smith, Betty. *A Tree Grows in Brooklyn.* New York: Harper, 1943. {3}

Smith, Charles R., Jr. *Perfect Harmony: A Musical Journey with the Boys Choir of Harlem.* New York: Hyperion, 2002. {1}

———. *Rimshots: Basketball Pix, Rolls, and Rhythms.* New York: Dutton, 1999. {1}

Sorel, Edward, and Cheryl Carlesimo. *The Saturday Kid.* New York: Margaret McElderry, 2000. {1}

Stein, Gertrude. *The World Is Round.* Illustrated by Clement Hurd. New York: Young Scott Books, 1939. {1}

Stewart, Sarah. *The Gardener.* Illustrated by David Small. New York: Farrar, Straus & Giroux, 1997. {1}

Swift, Hildegarde H. *The Little Red Lighthouse and the Great Gray Bridge.* Illustrated by Lynd Ward. New York: Harcourt, 1942. {1}

Tallchief, Maria, with Rosemary Wells. *Tallchief: America's Prima Ballerina.* Illustrated by Gary Kelley. New York: Viking, 1999. {1}

Taylor, Sydney. *All-of-a-Kind Family.* Illustrated by Helen John. Chicago: Follett, 1951. {2}

———. *All-of-a-Kind Family Uptown.* Illustrated by Mary Stevens. Chicago: Follett, 1958. {2}

Thomas, Pamela. *Brooklyn Pops Up.* Illustrated by Maurice Sendak, Robert Sabuda, et al. New York: Simon and Schuster, 2000. {1}

Thompson, Kay. *Eloise: A Book for Precocious Grownups.* Illustrated by Hilary Knight. New York: Simon and Schuster, 1955. {1}

Velasquez, Eric. *Grandma's Records.* New York: Walker, 2001. {1}

Vogel, Amos. *How Little Lori Visited Times Square.* Illustrated by Maurice Sendak. New York: Harper, 1963. {1}

Waber, Bernard. *Gina.* Boston: Houghton Mifflin, 1995. {1}

———. *The House on East 88th Street.* Boston: Houghton Mifflin, 1962. {1}

Waldman, Neil. *The Starry Night.* Honesdale, PA: Boyds Mills Press, 1999. {1}

———. *They Came from the Bronx: How the Buffalo Were Saved from Extinction.* Honesdale, PA: Boyds Mills Press, 2001. {1}

Walker, Alice. *Langston Hughes: American Poet.* Illustrated by Catherine Deeter. New York: Amistad/Harper, 2001. {1}

Waters, Kate, and Madeline Slovenz-Low. *Lion Dancer: Ernie Wan's Chinese New Year.* Photographed by Martha Cooper. New York: Scholastic, 1990. {1}

Weitzman, Jacqueline Preiss. *You Can't Take a Balloon into the Metropolitan Museum*. Illustrated by Robin Preiss Glasser. New York: Dial, 1998. {1}

White, E.B. *Stuart Little*. Illustrated by Garth Williams. New York: Harper, 1945. {2}

Wiesner, David. *Sector 7*. New York: Clarion, 1999. {1}

Wilder, Laura Ingalls. *Little House on the Prairie*. New York: Harper, 1935. {2}

Wilker, Josh. *The Lenape Indians*. New York and Philadelphia: Chelsea House, 1993. {2}

Williams, Vera B. *Scooter*. New York: Greenwillow, 1993. {2}

Williams-Garcia, Rita. *Fast Talk on a Slow Track*. New York: Lodestar, 1991. {3}

Woodson, Jacqueline. *Last Summer with Maizon*. New York: Delacorte, 1990. {3}

Yolen, Jane, ed. *Sky Scrape/City Scape*. Illustrated by Ken Condon. Honesdale, PA: Boyds Mills Press, 1996. {2}

Yorinks, Arthur. *Sid & Sol*. Illustrated by Richard Egielski. New York: Farrar, Straus & Giroux, 1977. {1}

Yue, Charlotte and David. *The Wigwam and the Longhouse*. Boston: Houghton Mifflin, 2000. {2}

Zindel, Paul. *The Pigman*. New York: Harper, 1968. {3}

———. *The Pigman & Me*. New York: HarperCollins, 1991. {3}

———. *Rats*. New York: Hyperion, 1999. {3}

Zolotow, Charlotte. *The Park Book*. Illustrated by H.A. Rey. New York: Harper, 1944. {1}

■

A Note on Sources

■

In the course of researching *Storied City*, I consulted a wide range of currently available reference works on various aspects of New York City history and contemporary life. Among the books most helpful to me were the following: *AIA Guide to New York City*, third edition, edited by Elliot Willensky and Norval White (San Diego: Harcourt Brace Jovanovich, 1988); *Bronx Accent: A Literary and Pictorial History of the Borough*, compiled by Lloyd Ultan and Barbara Unger (New Brunswick: Rutgers UP, 2000); *The Encyclopedia of New York City*, edited by Kenneth T. Jackson (New Haven, Yale UP, 1995); *Gotham: A History of New York City to 1898*, by Edwin G. Burrows and Mike Wallace (New York: Oxford UP, 1999); *The Neighborhoods of Brooklyn*, edited by Kenneth T. Jackson and John B. Manbeck (New Haven: Yale UP, 1998); and *Old Queens—N.Y. in Early Photographs*, by Vincent F. Seyfried and William Asadorian (New York: Dover, 1991).

Illustration Credits

■

The publisher and author wish to thank the following authors, illustrators, photographers, and publishers for granting permission to reproduce works and for their kind cooperation in the realization of this guide. (All photographs other than those on pages 20 & 64 were taken by Leonard S. Marcus.)

p.vi: *Stuart Little*, by E. B. White, illustrated by Garth Williams. Illustrations copyright renewed © 1973 by Garth Williams. Used by permission of HarperCollins Publishers. • p.4: *On the Day Peter Stuyvesant Sailed into Town*, by Arnold Lobel. Used by permission of the Estate of Arnold Lobel. • p.8: From *Little Toot*, by Hardie Gramatky, copyright 1939, renewed © 1967 by Hardie Gramatky. Used by permission of G. P. Putnam's Sons, A division of Penguin Young Readers Group, a member of Penguin Group (USA) Inc. All rights reserved. • p.10: From *Liberty!*, by Allan Drummond, copyright © 2002 by Allan Drummond. Reprinted by permission of Farrar, Straus and Giroux. • p.12: *Peppe the Lamplighter*, by Elisa Bartone, illustrated by Ted Lewin. Illustrations copyright © 1993 by Ted Lewin. Used by permission of Harper-Collins Publishers. • p.13: Illustration from *Chinatown* by William Low, © 1997 by William Low. Reprinted by permission of Henry Holt and Company, LLC. • p.14: Reprinted with the permission of Simon & Schuster Books for Young Readers, an imprint of Simon & Schuster Children's Publishing Division, from *When Zaydeh Danced on Eldridge Street*, by Elsa Okon Rael, illustrated by Marjorie Priceman. Illustrations copyright © 1997 Marjorie Priceman. • p.20: From *Rimshots: Basketball Pix, Rolls and Rhythms*, by Charles R. Smith Jr., copyright © 1999 by Charles R. Smith Jr. Used by permission of Dutton Children's Books, a division of Penguin Young Readers Group, a member of Penguin Group (USA) Inc. All rights reserved. • p.20: From *Bein' with You This Way*, by W. Nikola-Lisa, illustrated by Michael Bryant. Text copyright © 1994 by W. Nikola-Lisa. Illustrations copyright © 1994 by Michael Bryant. Reprinted by permission of Lee & Low Books. • p.21: *The Park Book*, by Charlotte Zolotow, illustrated by H. A. Rey. Illustrations by H. A. Rey, copyright 1944; renewed 1972, by the Estate of Margret and H. A. Rey. Reproduced by permission of the estate of Margret and H. A. Rey. • p.23: From *Madlenka*, by Peter Sís, copyright © 2000 by Peter Sís. Reprinted by permission of Farrar, Straus and Giroux. • p.24: From *The Gardener*, by Sarah Stewart, illustrated by David Small. Text copyright © 1997 by Sarah Stewart. Pictures copyright © 1997 by David Small. Reprinted by permission of Farrar, Straus and Giroux. • p.30: From *The Inside-Outside Book of New York City*, by Roxie Munro, copyright © 1985, renewed © 2001 by Roxie Munro. Reprinted by permission of SeaStar Books, a division of North-South Books Inc. • p.34: *The Pushcart War*, by Jean Merrill, illustrated by Ronni Solbert. Used by permission of HarperCollins Publishers. • p.40: From *Next Stop Grand Central*, by Maira Kalman, copyright © 1999 by Maira Kalman. Used by permission of G. P. Putnam's Sons, a division of Penguin Young Readers Group, a member of Penguin Group (USA) Inc. All rights reserved. • p.43: From *Roller Skates*, by Ruth Sawyer, illustrated by Valenti Angelo, copyright 1936 by Ruth Sawyer, renewed © 1964 by Ruth Sawyer Durand. Used by permission of Viking Penguin, a division of Penguin Young Readers Group, a member of Penguin Group (USA) Inc. All rights reserved. • p.45: From *Andy and the Lion*, by James Daugherty, copyright 1938 by James Daugherty, renewed © 1966 by James Daugherty. Used by permission of Viking Penguin, a division of Penguin Young Readers Group, a member of Penguin Group (USA) Inc. All rights reserved. • p.47: From *Chester Cricket's Pigeon Ride*, by George Selden, illustrated by Garth Williams. Text copyright © 1981 by George Selden. Pictures copyright ©

1981 by Garth Williams. Reprinted by permission of Farrar, Straus and Giroux. •
p.48: Cover from *James and the Giant Peach*, by Roald Dahl, (Puffin 1973). Text ©
Roald Dahl Nominee Ltd, 1961. Cover illustration © Quentin Blake, 2001. • p.49:
Illustration from *Sector 7*, by David Wiesner. Copyright © 1999 by David Wiesner.
Reprinted by permission of Clarion Books/Houghton Mifflin Company. All rights
reserved. • p.51: From *The Cricket in Times Square*, by George Selden, illustrated by
Garth Williams. Copyright © 1960 by George Selden Thompson and Garth
Williams. Reprinted by permission of Farrar, Straus and Giroux. • p.54: Text and
illustrations copyright © 1999 by Neil Waldman from *The Starry Night* by Neil
Waldman. Published by Caroline House/Boyds Mills Press, Inc. Reprinted by per-
mission. • p.55: Reprinted with the permission of Simon & Schuster Books for Young
Readers, an imprint of Simon & Schuster Children's Publishing Division, from *Eloise*,
by Kay Thompson, drawings by Hilary Knight. Copyright 1955 Kay Thompson;
copyright renewed © 1983 Kay Thompson. • p.57: From *One Sunday Morning*, by
Yumi Heo. Copyright © 1999 by Yumi Heo. Reprinted by permission of Scholastic
Inc. • p.58: From *My New York*, by Kathy Jakobsen. Copyright © 1993 by Kathy
Jakobsen. By permission of Little, Brown and Company, (Inc.) • p.59: *The Gingerbread
Boy*, by Richard Egielski. Copyright © 1997 by Richard Egielski. Used by permission
of HarperCollins Publishers. • p.63: Reprinted with the permission of Atheneum
Books for Young Readers, an imprint of Simon & Schuster Children's Publishing
Division, from *The Mixed-up Files of Mrs. Basil E. Frankweiler*, by E. L. Konigsburg.
Copyright © 1967 E. L. Konigsburg. • p.64: Photograph of the Fountain at the Met
by E. L. Konigsburg, courtesy of E. L. Konigsburg and The University of Pittsburgh.
• p.66: From *You Can't Take a Balloon Into the Metropolitan Museum*, by Jacqueline
Preiss Weitzman, illustrated by Robin Preiss Glasser, copyright © 1998 by Jacqueline
Preiss Weitzman and Robin Preiss Glasser. Used by permission of Dial Books for
Young Readers, a division of Penguin Young Readers Group, a member of Penguin
Group (USA) Inc. All rights reserved. • p.68: Illustration from *The House on East 88th
Street*, by Bernard Waber. Copyright © 1962, and renewed 1990 by Bernard Waber.
Reprinted by permission of Houghton Mifflin Company. All rights reserved. • p.69:
From *Harriet the Spy*, by Louise Fitzhugh, copyright © 1964 by Lois Anne Moore-
head. Used by permission of Random House Children's Books, a division of Random
House, Inc. • p.73: From *Under New York*, by Linda Oatman High, illustrated by
Robert Rayevsky. Text copyright © 2001 by Linda Oatman High. Illustrations copy-
right © 2001 by Robert Rayevsky. Reprinted by permission of Holiday House. • p.75:
From *The Dinosaurs of Waterhouse Hawkins*, by Barbara Kerley, illustrated by Brian
Selznick. Illustrations copyright © 2001 by Brian Selznick. Reprinted by permission
of Scholastic Inc. • p.76: *The Philharmonic Gets Dressed*, by Karla Kuskin, illustrated by
Marc Simont. Illustrations copyright © 1982 by Marc Simont. Used by permission of
HarperCollins Publishers. • p.77: From *Pet of the Met*, by Lydia and Don Freeman,
copyright 1953 by Lydia and Don Freeman, renewed © 1981 by Lydia Freeman.
Used by permission of Viking Penguin, a division of Penguin Young Readers Group,
a member of Penguin Group (USA) Inc. All rights reserved. • p.89: Illustration from
Uptown, by Bryan Collier, © 2000 by Bryan Collier. Reprinted by permission of
Henry Holt and Company, LLC. • p.91: From *Tar Beach*, by Faith Ringgold, copyright
© 1991 by Faith Ringgold. Used by permission of Crown Publishers, an imprint of
Random House Children's Books, a division of Random House, Inc. • p.92: From *Love
to Langston*, by Tony Medina, illustrated by R. Gregory Christie. Text copyright ©
2002 by Tony Medina. Illustrations copyright © 2002 by R. Gregory Christie.
Reprinted by permission of Lee & Low Books. • p.96: Illustration from *The Little Red
Lighthouse and the Great Gray Bridge*, by Hildegarde H. Swift and Lynd Ward, copyright 1942 by Harcourt, Inc. and renewed 1970 by Hildegarde H. Swift and Lynd
Ward, reprinted by permission of the publisher. • p.101: *Harbor*, by Donald Crews.

Used by permission of HarperCollins Publishers. • p.102: Reprinted with the permission of Atheneum Books for Young Readers, an imprint of Simon & Schuster Children's Publishing Division, from *Brooklyn Bridge*, by Lynn Curlee. Copyright © 2001 Lynn Curlee. • p.103: From *Hattie and the Wild Waves*, by Barbara Cooney, copyright © 1990 by Barbara Cooney. Used by permission of Viking Penguin, a division of Penguin Young Readers Group, a member of Penguin Group (USA) Inc. All rights reserved. • p.108: From *A Teeny Tiny Baby*, by Amy Schwartz. Copyright © 1994 by Amy Schwartz. Reprinted by permission of Orchard Books, an imprint of Scholastic Inc. • p.110: From *Gowanus Dogs*, by Jonathan Frost. Copyright © 1999 by Jonathan Frost. Reprinted by permission of Farrar, Straus and Giroux. • p.116: Text and illustrations copyright © 2001 by Neil Waldman from *They Came from the Bronx*, by Neil Waldman. Published by Caroline House/Boyds Mills Press, Inc. Reprinted by permission. • p.117: Illustrations from *Home Run: The Story of Babe Ruth*, by Robert Burleigh, illustrations copyright © 1998 by Mike Wimmer, reproduced by permission of Harcourt, Inc. • p.122: *Jackson Heights: From Ice Age to Space Age*, by Rudolph E. Greco, Jr., and Claudia Solomon, illustrated by Queens schoolchildren. Text copyright © 1996 by Rudolph E. Greco, Jr. Published by the Jackson Heights Beautification Group. • p.122: Taken from *Cowboy Dreams*, copyright © 1990 by the Estate of Dayal Kaur Khalsa, published by Tundra Books. • p.123: From *Abuela*, by Arthur Dorros, illustrated by Elisa Kleven. Illustrations copyright © 1991 by Elisa Kleven. Used by permission of Dutton Children's Books, a division of Penguin Young Readers Group, a member of Penguin Group (USA) Inc. All rights reserved. • p.124: *Mama, Coming and Going*, by Judith Caseley. Illustrations copyright © 1994 by Judith Caseley. Used by permission of HarperCollins. • p.127: From *Edna*, by Robert Burleigh, illustrated by Joanna Yardley. Illustration copyright © 2000 by Joanna Yardley. Reprinted by permission of Orchard Books, an imprint of Scholastic Inc. • p.154: *The Park Book*, by Charlotte Zolotow, illustrated by H. A. Rey. Illustrations by H. A. Rey, copyright 1944; renewed 1972, by the estate of Margret and H. A. Rey. Reproduced by permission of the estate of Margret and H. A. Rey.

Index

∎

The Park Book,
by Charlotte Zolotow,
illustrated by H.A. Rey